Essential Java
for AP CompSci

From Programming to Computer Science

Doug Winnie

Apress®

Essential Java for AP CompSci: From Programming to Computer Science

Doug Winnie
Mission Hills, KS, USA

ISBN-13 (pbk): 978-1-4842-6182-8   ISBN-13 (electronic): 978-1-4842-6183-5
https://doi.org/10.1007/978-1-4842-6183-5

Managing Director, Apress Media LLC: Welmoed Spahr
Acquisitions Editor: Steve Anglin
Development Editor: Matthew Moodie
Coordinating Editor: Mark Powers

Cover designed by eStudioCalamar
Cover image by Devin Avery on Unsplash (www.unsplash.com)

Distributed to the book trade worldwide by Apress Media, LLC, 1 New York Plaza, New York, NY 10004, U.S.A. Phone 1-800-SPRINGER, fax (201) 348-4505, e-mail orders-ny@springer-sbm.com, or visit www.springeronline.com. Apress Media, LLC is a California LLC and the sole member (owner) is Springer Science + Business Media Finance Inc (SSBM Finance Inc). SSBM Finance Inc is a **Delaware** corporation.

For information on translations, please e-mail editorial@apress.com; for reprint, paperback, or audio rights, please e-mail bookpermissions@springernature.com.

Apress titles may be purchased in bulk for academic, corporate, or promotional use. eBook versions and licenses are also available for most titles. For more information, reference our Print and eBook Bulk Sales web page at http://www.apress.com/bulk-sales.

Any source code or other supplementary material referenced by the author in this book is available to readers on GitHub via the book's product page, located at www.apress.com/9781484261828. For more detailed information, please visit http://www.apress.com/source-code.

Printed on acid-free paper

For Mike, and all of the great decisions we have made together.

Table of Contents

About the Author

Doug Winnie has been teaching programming in the classroom or with online videos for over 15 years. Online, his videos have over two million views on Adobe, Lynda.com, and LinkedIn Learning. Doug's courses cover topics like computer science principles, Java, C#, JavaScript, product management fundamentals, virtual machines, and other products and technologies.

He has written two books on programming and collaboration between user experience designers and developers.

Currently, he is the Chief Learning Officer at MentorNations, an international nonprofit focused on evolving digital literacy and entrepreneurial skills across the world.

Previously, Doug was head of community for the LinkedIn Learning instructor organization, representing the interests of over 1400 teachers and instructors worldwide. He was an internal contributor to the Windows Insider Program and part of a global initiative at Microsoft to teach 7.6 billion people around the world digital coding and programming literacy skills. He was also a LinkedIn Culture Champion, working with LinkedIn employees around the globe to put on employee cultual events on special days called InDays.

Earlier, Doug was a principal product manager at Adobe and specialized working on new products for the user experience, interactive design, and web design audiences.

You can find out more about Doug on his LinkedIn profile:

www.linkedin.com/in/sfdesigner

About the Technical Reviewer

Jeff Friesen is a freelance teacher and software developer with an emphasis on Java. In addition to authoring *Java I/O, NIO and NIO.2* (Apress) and *Java Threads and the Concurrency Utilities* (Apress), Jeff has written numerous articles on Java and other technologies (such as Android) for JavaWorld (`JavaWorld.com`), InformIT (`InformIT.com`), `Java.net`, SitePoint (`SitePoint.com`), and other websites. Jeff can be contacted via his website at `JavaJeff.ca` or via his LinkedIn profile (`www.linkedin.com/in/javajeff`).

SPRINT 1

Introduction

Computer science has become a basic life skill that everyone is going to need to learn. Whether you are going into a career or side hustle in business, technology, creativity, architecture, or almost any other field, you will find programming, coding, and computer science play a role.

In fact, if you look at the top skills on LinkedIn for the United States, in the last year all ten of the top were programming, computer science, or code related. These include cloud and distributed computing, statistical analysis, data mining, mobile development, storage systems management, user interface design, network and information security, middleware and integration software, web architecture and development frameworks, algorithm design, and Java development.[1]

What is unique about computer science is how it has become a skill, and not just a career. While there are jobs and titles of "Computer Scientist," the skill of computer science, and specifically coding and programming, is almost everywhere.

In marketing, you need to analyze and sift through tons of user data and metrics on how people use your products, website, apps, or services. In medicine, doctors and researchers need to gather and analyze data gathered from clinical studies or to find new breakthroughs. In agriculture and farming, thousands of IoT devices need to be deployed and managed to gather data on soil conditions, humidity, and crop health. In architecture and construction, mapping out and analyzing how people use elevators, building infrastructure, or public spaces can help design better buildings for people to work and live in. Even when building a side business, or "hustle," entrepreneurs may need to perform research, build a website, program a mobile app or game, or perform tons of different activities involving code, logic, automation, and programming.

---

[1]"The Top 10 Skills You Will Be Hiring For in 2017," https://business.linkedin.com/talent-solutions/blog/trends-and-research/2016/linkedin-new-report-reveals-the-latest-job-seeking-trends

© Doug Winnie 2021
D. Winnie, *Essential Java for AP CompSci*, https://doi.org/10.1007/978-1-4842-6183-5_1

When people create projects based on code, they organize their work into multiple chunks or segments of development. They call these "sprints." So, we will learn Java in the same way, using multiple sprints that will teach a single topic to help us keep pace with things along the way. Part of what makes learning coding difficult is it can be difficult to find real-world examples to draw parallels from. If you are planning on taking the AP Exam in Computer Science, many of the questions will not have any real-world context and will require you to understand and follow code without that as a reference.

For you, this can make it confusing, but just remember: there are two sides to programming—what is being done and how it happens.

The "what" is pretty easy, and this gives the code context, like parsing transit data, rolling a virtual die, or adding sales data for a quarter together.

"How" it happens is a completely different story however. This is where you need to break things down into individual steps and start to think like a computer. A computer is going to think only about one single step at a time. It has no concept of what comes next or what came before it. It only is concerned with the present. So, if it can't find something—you get an error. If it tries to do something that doesn't exist—you get an error. If you try doing something out of order—you guessed it, you get an error.

In fact, the computer is pretty dumb. I mean, like really dumb. What makes it smart is how we are able to string multiple actions together to make something work. And with growing advances in artificial intelligence, the computer itself can start making adjustments. And then Skynet activates, and we all know what happens after that.

So when we learn programming, we are going to focus on three things:

- What is the process

- What is the syntax

- What is the flow

The process is represented as a flowchart. We will learn how to make these to help you plan out what you are going to do before you write a line of code. At first, the flowcharts will be pretty simple, but then they will get more complex. And yep, you will get pretty annoyed with flowcharts before the year is over, but trust me...they help.

The syntax is the code; this is what you write that translates the process you create in a flowchart to the instructions that the computer can understand.

Finally, there is the flow. This is where you trace through the code and see how the data and information it stores along the way changes, and you can see how the operation of the program cascades from line to line. You will be building charts that will capture the programming flow so you can better understand how the computer processes code to make your next program easier to conceive and code.

What You Need

You will need a Windows or macOS computer to complete the projects in this book. You will need to install and configure the Java JDK (Java Development Kit) and IntelliJ from JetBrains (our IDE or code editor for the class). If you are on macOS, it is suggested that you uninstall the built-in Java JRE (Java Runtime Environment) and use the one included in the Oracle Java JDK. This will avoid warnings that appear when you build your projects.

Setting Up the Java JDK and IntelliJ

To get started with our exercises, we need to set up our computers to work with Java code and run it. This is called creating a development environment.

As you learn more about coding and programming, you will encounter many different tools to help you do your job. There are so many in fact, that you might find that one fits better than another. While they all essentially do the same thing, there are features and options in different tools that mesh better with different types of coders.

Coding Tools and IDEs

Coding tools, and their more sophisticated brothers, the integrated development environment, or IDE, can sometimes spark passionate debate on which one is considered "the best," but ultimately it comes down to you, the coder, to decide what is best for you.

To help make this course and the tools we use easy to understand and the same across Windows and macOS, the tool we will use is **IntelliJ IDEA**. IDEA is a free coding tool from JetBrains that is easy to use, not very complicated, and it is the same across platforms.

There are others that you can use for this course as well. Some examples are Eclipse or NetBeans. These tools provide the same features, but I wouldn't recommend using them to help us all be consistent with our tools when working together.

The other key tool you will need is the **Java Development Kit** or JDK. In order for the IDE to work, it needs to have the Java compiler to create your Java bytecode and then use the Java Runtime Environment or JRE to run your program in a virtual machine, called the JVM.

© Doug Winnie 2021
D. Winnie, *Essential Java for AP CompSci*, https://doi.org/10.1007/978-1-4842-6183-5_2

The version that you will use is the Java SE or Standard Edition that you can download for free from Oracle. Regardless if you use IDEA, or another IDE, you will need to install the JDK in order to compile and build your programs.

Installation and Setup

If you want to follow along with the same tools that I'll be using, you will need to install the JDK and IntelliJ IDEA.

To install the tools I'm using, you will need a PC with Windows 7, 8, 8.1, or 10 already installed.

For a macOS computer, you will need Yosemite, High Sierra, or Mojave. It is recommended that you uninstall the version that Apple installs by default (called OpenJDK). Refer to instructions online for how to do this.

Install the JDK

First, we need to install the JDK.

With your browser, go to the Oracle website:

`www.oracle.com/technetwork/java/javase/downloads/index.html`

From here, click the Java JDK download button.

Then accept the license agreement, and then select Windows which must be installed on a 64-bit computer and operating system or for macOS.

Your browser will prompt you to save the installer to your computer. Save and run the installer using the defaults for the configuration.

Remember the location of where the JDK is installed; you will need this later on to connect IntelliJ IDEA to the JDK.

Install IntelliJ

Now we need to install IntelliJ IDEA.

With your browser, go to the JetBrains website:

`www.jetbrains.com`

Under Tools, look for the column IDEs, and select IntelliJ IDEA. We will use the Community Edition, which is free.

Your browser will prompt you to save the installer to your computer. Click Save to continue and download.

Run the installer and accept the defaults for all the settings.

That's it! IntelliJ IDEA and the Java Development Kit are successfully installed!

Setting Up GitHub

When you code, you need to have a location to store it and share that code with others to work with it and review it. Tools called code repositories are ideal ways to do this, and there are several different types that are available for developers to use; one of the most popular is GitHub, and we will explore it here. GitHub, in the context of this book, is a tool that you can use on your own. I'm introducing it here, because as you get more familiar with programming, you'll find it to be an indispensable tool.

GitHub

The one that we will use is called GitHub. GitHub is a free public code platform that developers use to build, archive, and manage coding projects for individual or group collaboration. It is built on the Git technology that is ordinarily used for private, internal projects, but GitHub builds their public platform on Git to make it available to anyone.

To create a GitHub account is simple. Go to `www.github.com/` and create an account there. For our use in class, please create your account as your Serra email address so I can easily identify your account.

When you create your account, be sure to go to GitHub Desktop to download the desktop client for Windows or macOS. You can download the installer here: `https://desktop.github.com/`.

Install the client and sign in to your account. You can then create a repository to keep track of the changes you make in your classwork projects. You can create a single project to capture all of your homework assignments, or you can create an individual repository for each project. Whichever you choose is up to you.

© Doug Winnie 2021
D. Winnie, *Essential Java for AP CompSci*, https://doi.org/10.1007/978-1-4842-6183-5_3

How GitHub Works

GitHub and Git create a special directory that it uses to keep track of all changes that you make to the files inside of it. When you make a change to a file, it tracks what the change was and notes that.

This is different than a backup. A backup creates a copy of everything that is in a folder. A change in Git and GitHub only records what changed, which can save a lot of space and is much faster to process.

There are many advanced workflows and automations that you can tie into Git and GitHub, but we will only be using the platform to store and share projects and homework assignments.

There are ways to tie in GitHub directly into the IntelliJ IDEA IDE, but for simplicity, we can use the GitHub Desktop client to make, track, commit, and sync changes to our GitHub account.

Lifecycle of a Repository

A repository, or repo, starts with the master branch, sometimes known as a trunk. For individual developers, or small teams, projects might only use a master branch and never create alternate versions of it.

As the program evolves and new changes are made, they are saved to the repository by making a commit. A commit contains the changes to the code and a brief comment and description made by the developer on what changed for future reference. Over time, there will be dozens or hundreds of commits on a repository.

At some point, a repository will need to split in some way. Either there needs to be simultaneous work and they don't want to have code conflict with others, or a project needs to maintain an existing version and they want to do something else with it. In that case, a branch is created from the main trunk, and development can happen in parallel with the original code.

At some point, a branch will need to rejoin the main development, and this is done by merging that branch back into the master trunk.

For open source repositories, it is common for a developer to find a helpful framework and want to add it to their own development environment. To do that, they would fork the repository, creating a copy in their own environment to work with and potentially make changes.

When a developer makes changes or improvements to a forked repository, they might want to contribute those changes back to the main repository they forked from. To do that, they submit a pull request back to the original repository. As part of this pull request, the developer outlines the changes that were made, and the person who receives the requests can compare the proposed changes to the repo by performing a diff that shows the changes side by side from one another.

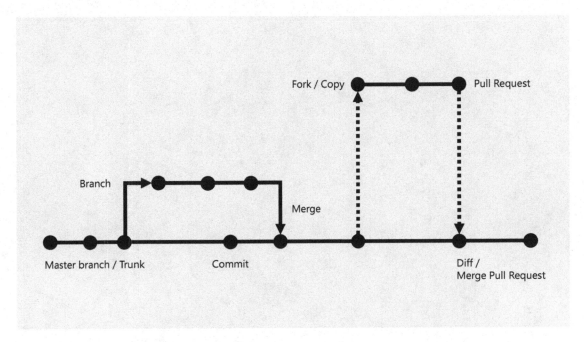

Figure 3-1. *Repository lifecycle*

Repositories can vary in complexity from something very simple with a single or a handful of developers to a large open source project with tens of thousands of developers. Code repos are the core of how software developers work together on projects of any size.

SPRINT 4

Programming Languages

Programming languages started as an abstract concept and then adapted and changed over time. From the origins of machine language, switch input, extending into the early days of simple line-by-line coding like COBOL or BASIC to object-oriented languages like Java and C#, to quantum computer languages like Q#, the evolution of programming languages has developed over the course of many decades.

Origin of Programming

In the early 1840s, Charles Babbage proposed a machine called the Analytical Engine. It was only a proposal—no actual machine was built, but one inventive woman by the name of Ada Lovelace decided to write an article that provided detailed instructions on how to represent Bernoulli [ber-noo-li] numbers, a recursive equation based on number theory, on the Analytical Engine. This article is considered to be the very first computer program.

Since then the devices that can be programmed went from theoretical to physical, manual to automatic, analog to digital. With each evolutionary step, the way we program computers needed to evolve as well.

With the birth of mainframe computers, data processing required instructions to be sent to the machine to process and interpret the instructions from the programmer. This was then applied to data to organize and analyze the data. Instructions were entered through a keyboard, but without the benefit of a monitor, so everything was done through printouts on paper or storing data in the form of punched holes on cards that were stored in stacks. If you look carefully at text encodings and at some programming languages, you'll see things like "carriage return" or "print" that are carryovers from those printer days from decades ago.

13

© Doug Winnie 2021
D. Winnie, *Essential Java for AP CompSci*, https://doi.org/10.1007/978-1-4842-6183-5_4

As computers got smaller and more powerful, more languages were created. Languages also were created to serve specific types of projects and industries like mathematics and science, data storage, and graphics.

Today, we work with programming languages that can serve many different purposes. In fact, a programmer often needs to use multiple programming languages to get a project completed. As languages have evolved, they have become specialized to complete specific tasks. As a programmer, you will use the best languages for specific tasks and combine them together to create your project.

The programming languages you learn today will continue to evolve and change in the future. With future waves of new technology, new languages will be developed to allow programmers to drive even more innovation.

Forms of Programming

As programming has evolved over the decades, the types of programming you can do have changed as well. Depending on what you want to do, there are different types or forms of programming languages that work in different ways. As a programmer, some forms of programming give you direct access to the computer processor, while others abstract the hardware into more human language that needs to be translated or converted into the native language of the hardware. Here are some example forms of programming that you might encounter.

Machine Language

Machine languages allow programmers to code instructions directly to the processor or hardware. Processors can be programmed by sending sequences and patterns of ones and zeros through the processor to enable actions to take place. As a result, the code that is entered by the programmer is almost natively written. Assembly language, which is an abstraction of machine language, uses special codes to modify processor registers and perform functions.

Interpreted

Interpreted languages are readable by humans more easily than assembly or machine languages. The programmer writes the code and then runs it. A component called an interpreter reads each line of code and then "interprets" it into native instructions for

14

the computer. The process is much slower than machine language since the interpreter needs to convert each instruction provided by the programmer, even if it repeats a line of code multiple times—it needs to interpret it each time. JavaScript is an example of an interpreted language. A programmer can stop the execution of the program, make a change to a line, and then run it again without any other steps.

Compiled

A compiled language takes instructions written by a human and sends that code to something called a compiler. A compiler takes the program instructions and converts it to binary bytecode or native code for the hardware and creates a program called an executable. This program is native to the hardware and operating system and can't easily be converted back to the original programmed instructions. With the code now in the native computer format, it runs much faster than interpreted code, but if you need to make a change, you need to adjust the original program instructions and recompile it to create a new executable. If you are creating programs for multiple types of processors, you need to compile unique versions for each native instruction code for the target platforms. C is an example of a compiled language.

Object-Oriented

Object-oriented programming, or OOP, treats everything as an object. An object can store values; perform actions, called methods; and accept and return values. An object is defined using a template, called a class, that defines what an object can do. A programmer can then create an instance of that class that has all of the capabilities defined by the class. Java and C# are examples of object-oriented languages.

Data

There are languages that are specifically designed at working with data. One example is SQL, pronounced as see-quel, which is a language designed for working with databases. This is a query language, where you ask a database a question and it gives you a set of data as a result. You can use SQL to combine multiple databases together to create combinations that you can then analyze. R is another example of a data language. R is designed for statistical computing and graphing.

Functional

Functional programming approaches programming in a much different way. Think of it like this: In a traditional programming language, which is called imperative, you are defining the state of a value, object, or component. You create and define tasks to complete, called an algorithm, that go from beginning to end. Functional programming isn't bound by an algorithm. In a functional language, you perform transformations on values, like a function in mathematics. You take a value or object and modify it, with the ability to string multiple transformations together using functions. Functional languages focus on what needs to be done, without much care for how it is performed. Examples of functional languages include Haskell, Scala, and F#.

Scripting

Operating systems regularly need to execute commands to configure servers, install software, or perform maintenance. To automate that process, there are scripting languages that allow systems like Windows, Linux, and macOS to save common commands as a script that can be run multiple times or distributed to multiple computers. PowerShell, perl, and bash are examples of scripting languages.

As you can see, there are multiple types of programming languages that you can work with to perform different types of tasks. This course will focus on concepts found in object-oriented, compiled, and interpreted languages like JavaScript, Java, C#, and Swift.

History and Uses of Java

Java started off with lofty goals, and today it is one of the most popular and widely used languages throughout the world.

Java Beginnings

Java got its start at Sun Microsystems and was first released to the public in 1995. The development of the language started in 1991 by James Gosling, Mike Sheridan, and Patrick Naughton and was designed to be similar to C and C++ to help developers use their existing programming skills for the new language. Sun Microsystems was acquired by Oracle in 2009.

During development, Java was originally called Oak, then renamed Green, and finally released as Java from Java coffee, which is why the logo for Java is of a steaming coffee cup.

Write once, run anywhere

When it was launched, it promised "write once, run anywhere," meaning that programs you created in Java only needed to be coded once, and they could run on any platform that supported Java.

Java's Primary Goals

From the very beginning, there were five primary goals in the creation of the Java language:

1. It must be "simple, object-oriented, and familiar."

2. It must be "robust and secure."

© Doug Winnie 2021
D. Winnie, *Essential Java for AP CompSci*, https://doi.org/10.1007/978-1-4842-6183-5_5

3. It must be "architecture-neutral and portable."

4. It must execute with "high performance."

5. It must be "interpreted, threaded, and dynamic."

Today, Java is one of the most popular languages in use. Java's heavy use in web applications, enterprise desktop applications with technologies like JavaFX, and the Android ecosystem makes it a great language to learn with many flexible ways to use it.

Uses of Java

Since Java was first released, it has grown to power many large-scale web applications for ecommerce, finance, and other industries. Java applications are built on the server side and connect to web servers to handle the business logic of applications.

Java is also the core language of Android, and native applications created using Google's Android Studio tools are built using the Java language. In addition, you'll find Java embedded in many devices, like televisions and other consumer electronics.

Many frameworks have been created based on the Java programming language to accelerate the development of applications across many platforms and devices.

For web applications, frameworks like Struts, JSF, Grails, Spring, and others are used individually or in combination with each other to provide scalable web apps that can support millions of customers.

For desktop applications, frameworks like JavaFX allow developers to create user interfaces using FXML, an XML-based markup language, and meld that with Java code.

For mobile, the Android SDK from Google contains a tool for developing Android apps and an emulator to deploy and run your app on a virtual device for testing.

As a developer, there are many coding tools available to you for Java. Integrated development environments, or IDEs, help combine many of the tasks you need to perform like coding, code management, debugging, working with code repositories, and creating documentation. Some of the more popular IDEs are IntelliJ IDEA, Eclipse, and NetBeans. The one we will be using in this course is from IntelliJ.

Java opens up almost unlimited opportunities for you as a developer, and the best thing is that Java is not complicated to learn or understand once you get past the basics. Using your new Java skills, you can build apps for almost anything.

How Java Works

Java is a unique programming language due to the "write once, run anywhere" mantra that was part of the original vision. How it makes this vision come to life is important to understanding how you work as a programmer.

The Problem with Compiled Languages

Compiled programming languages generally have a big limitation. When you convert your code to an executable program, the compiler reads the code and creates a binary file that is specific to a processor architecture.

So, if I used a language like C or C++ to compile a program on my 32-bit Windows PC, that program can't run on a Mac, nor can it run on a 64-bit Windows PC natively without added technologies to bridge the gap. It can only run on a 32-bit Windows PC.

Every processor and operating system is expecting a program to meet extremely specific requirements. The way the program accesses the hardware is vastly different between Intel processors, ARM-based processors (like those found on phones and tablets), and other processor types like RISC architectures. (Older Macs used this type of architecture using chips called PowerPC chips like the G5 or G4.)

Even 32-bit Intel processors and 64-bit Intel processors operate completely differently. So 64-bit programs can't run on 32-bit computers, and 32-bit programs can't run natively on 64-bit computers without additional software to make it compatible.

When you expand to other types of computers like servers, the number of processor types and architectures can get even more complex.

Web and application servers can use vastly different architecture types like Sparc, Xeon, Itanium, and other types over the last couple of decades.

So, the folks at Sun Microsystems, when they designed Java, wanted to get past this limitation, so they created an innovative way to get around it.

19

© Doug Winnie 2021
D. Winnie, *Essential Java for AP CompSci*, https://doi.org/10.1007/978-1-4842-6183-5_6

The JVM and JRE

When you run a Java program, you aren't just running the program, you are running a few things at the same time.

For multiple platforms, Oracle has created a set of technologies called the Java Runtime Environment and the Java Virtual Machine. These are built so that the specific architectures of the hardware including Intel, ARM, 64-bit, 32-bit, and more can run Java programs.

These runtimes are installed on the system and stay resident, waiting for a Java program to be executed.

When a Java program is called to run, the Java Runtime Environment, or JRE, kicks in and opens the compiled program. The runtime environment then captures the instructions of the program and converts them to native executions on the computer.

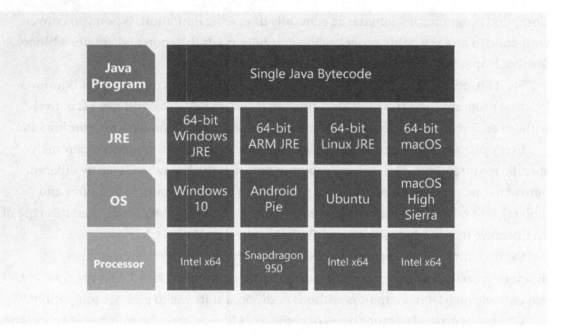

Java Program	Single Java Bytecode			
JRE	64-bit Windows JRE	64-bit ARM JRE	64-bit Linux JRE	64-bit macOS
OS	Windows 10	Android Pie	Ubuntu	macOS High Sierra
Processor	Intel x64	Snapdragon 950	Intel x64	Intel x64

This is what has made Java so universal. Wherever Oracle has created a JRE, you can run Java programs.

Compiling Java Bytecode

When you create your Java program, there are a few things in play when you create your code, called source code or source.

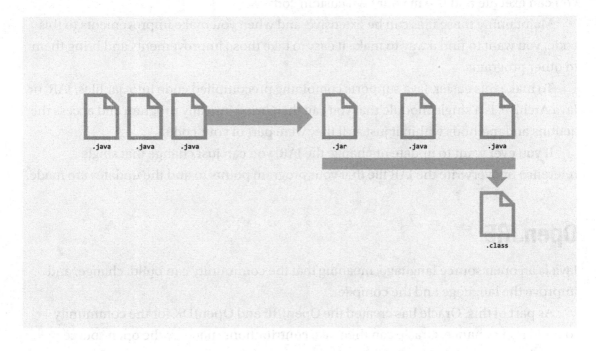

First, when you create your program, you are writing a plain text file. There are no formatting, special characters, graphics, or anything other than letters and numbers. When you save this file to your computer, it is a .java file, meaning that the file extension is .java.

When you are finished coding your program, you take the file and send it to the compiler. The compiler takes the instructions you created and converts them to Java Bytecode, which the JRE can read and understand. The Java Bytecode (sometimes referred to as JBC) is a concise and compressed file that isn't human readable but is designed to be understood and executed quickly by the JRE.

The JRE then takes those bytecode instructions and sends them to the native hardware to execute the program on the machine.

When you compile your program, you are creating these Java Bytecode files, called .class files, and they will run in the JRE against the native hardware of the architecture.

Precompiled Files

Sometimes, you will want to have files that you use repeatedly in your program. These generally are sections of code that will never change but contain prebuilt actions that you can execute and use in your own custom code.

Maintaining these files can be extensive, and when you make improvements to this code, you want to find a way to make it easy to take those improvements and bring them to other programs.

To make this easier, Java supports combining precompiled code into .jar files. JAR, or Java Archive, is a single module that you can then bring into any program and access the actions and methods within it just as if they were part of your code.

If you ever want to update or change the JAR, you can just change that single reference or overwrite the JAR file that your program points to and the updates are made.

OpenJRE

Java is an open source language, meaning that the community can build, change, and improve the language and the compiler.

As part of this, Oracle has created the OpenJRE and OpenJDK for the community to build and enhance. Oracle can then take contributions made by the open source community and bring them into the official Oracle Java JDK and JRE.

Oracle then adds additional security and other protections to ensure the applications that run on it are safe and secure. Because it is a packaged platform, this security is applied to any hardware, server, or cloud infrastructures.

Android is largely built on Java, and starting with Android N, or Android Nougat, Google switched to the OpenJDK due to litigation with Oracle.

In the end, to you, it doesn't matter which version of Java you are running. When you install any JDK and JRE, the source code, compiled files, and execution of the programs are essentially the same.

Flowcharting

Programming and coding are just as much about thinking and planning as it is about sitting in front of a keyboard. Often, a developer needs to plot out in their mind or on paper how a program is going to work. This can make the coding process much easier, especially if you are working together with others on a project.

A flowchart is a common way to sketch out your program. It is exactly as it sounds: a chart that visually shows the flow of a program. In a flowchart, you connect various steps, decisions, and actions together into a string that follows the flow of how the program will operate.

Because the computer is so literal with how it processes your actions and code, a flowchart makes it easier to code more accurately the first time vs. having to debug and thrash your way through code. Trust me, it is tempting to ditch the flowchart and go straight to the code, but if you are new, or relatively new to coding, it will save you a ton of time and force you to stop, pause, and sketch things out before you go to the keyboard.

Flowcharting Tools

There are a bunch of flowcharting tools you can use; some are pen and paper, and some are online.

Paper

Just like how a writer journals in a notebook, or a designer sketches in a sketchbook, a developer can often sketch a flowchart using pen and paper. Sometimes making things tangible and tactile helps slow your brain down and be more thoughtful with your code and program.

If you want to go with the paper approach, you can get a stencil to help with your work. It helps make things a bit cleaner.

23

© Doug Winnie 2021
D. Winnie, *Essential Java for AP CompSci*, https://doi.org/10.1007/978-1-4842-6183-5_7

Tablet and Stylus

If you have a tablet or laptop that supports a stylus like an iPad, Surface, or 2-in-1 laptop, there are lots of sketching apps that you can use for your flowcharting including OneNote, Adobe Illustrator Draw, Autodesk SketchBook, and more. Some specialized tablet apps can even detect the shapes you draw and convert them to template shapes.

Apps

Apps like OmniGraffle, Sketch, Adobe XD, Visio, PowerPoint, and Illustrator are examples of apps you can download or purchase and use to build your flowcharts. These apps vary in what they can do, but they all can work for building a flowchart.

I use Visio a lot, and it has a cool feature where you can create the steps for your flowchart in Excel and then import them into Visio to automatically create the flowchart. You can then resync the chart if you make changes in Excel.

Flowcharting Basics

Flowcharts use different shapes to represent unique types of steps in the program or process flow. These shapes then determine what steps are being taken and can also affect the direction the program flow can take.

Terminus

A basic flowchart starts with the pill shape; this is called a terminus shape and is used when you start and end your flowchart. Inside, you write in either "Start" or "Stop" and can optionally define how the program does this in the shape.

Then you draw a line, with an arrow, pointing to the next step in the flowchart.

Process/Action

An action, sometimes called a process, is represented by a simple rectangle. You create a single rectangle for every individual step that needs to be part of your program. We often combine multiple steps in our mind and think of them as a single action. So, something simple might seem like a single step, but it involves multiple actions.

You then create more steps in your flowchart and connect them using lines with arrows. They can turn and twist. They can be vertical or horizontal. It is entirely up to you.

Input and Output

In your program, you will often need to get input from the user or display output to them. These steps are represented by a parallelogram to distinguish them from other steps, and you describe it like any other action.

Decisions

Decisions branch the flow of a program based on the results of a question. The question must be answered with a "Yes" or "No" response. (You'll find out why later in the class).

A decision step uses a diamond shape and has two paths that come off of it. One for "Yes"; one for "No." You then connect these paths to different actions based on the results of the question.

These separate paths may reconnect at a later point, but that is all based on your program and when you want to make that happen.

Annotations

Sometimes you can't fit everything into a shape, so it is fine to add annotations or notes to the flowchart. These can either be added descriptions or details about the step or programming and coding notes for you or others when the coding starts.

Other Shapes

There are other shapes for working with data, creating subprocesses, and other actions, but we will cover those later when we need them. For now, we will stick with these four basic shapes.

Take Out the Trash

Let's take a look at an example flowchart, and you can see how this all comes together.

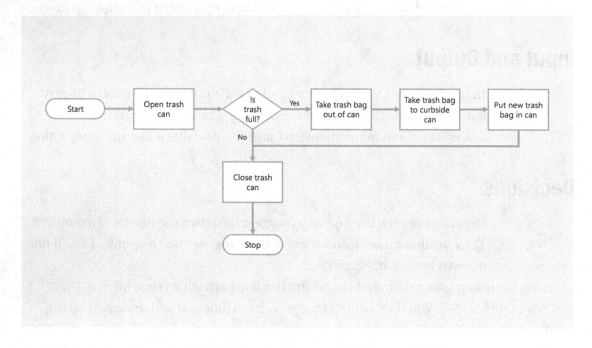

The flowchart starts with a terminus, or terminal shape, labeled start.

Then an action is performed, "Open trash can."

Next, we reach a decision. The answer to the question needs to be yes or no. "Is the trash full?" If it is, you follow the yes path. If it isn't, you follow the no path.

Depending on the path you take, you will continue from step to step following each action.

This chart has the decision paths meet back up to a single point, which is totally fine with a flowchart.

It then ends with the stop terminus.

But Is It Really That Simple?

No. It isn't. Because we make assumptions all the time, and often those assumptions lead us into problems.

Part of a programmer's job is to take complicated tasks and break them down into individual steps that can't be broken down any further.

It is like looking at water and drilling down to the molecules and then the atoms that form it. You dive down to the smallest element that forms the basis of the object. Now take that principle and apply it to an action. We take for granted many steps that are part of a group of actions.

Let's look at our previous example. Let's take out the trash.

The phrase "take out the trash" probably conjures up a few things in your mind. If someone tells me, "Hey Doug, can you take out the trash please?", there are certain steps that already form in my head around what I have to do.

For my home, these are the steps I need to do.

First, I need to go to the kitchen and grab the full garbage bag out of the trash can, then I take it around the house and empty the smaller trash cans in the bedroom and bathroom into it. Then I take it to the curbside can and put it inside.

That's it! I took out the trash.

But are those all of the steps? Did I break down everything enough to make sure that everything happens that needs to happen? What if I took the steps I mentioned and wrote them down and had someone follow them to the letter? Would they do what I expected?

No, they probably wouldn't, because even with those steps there are some assumptions that I didn't think of. For instance, if it is the day before trash pickup, I need to put the curbside can on the street. When I say "trash," I see it as trash and recycling, but someone who would take me literally might not see that.

As a programmer, you need to be as accurate and literal as possible with your code. Breaking down actions into smaller actions is critical to being successful. With each line of code that you write, like "take out the trash," you need to define each statement or action that needs to happen within that to fulfill everything that you expect and for the action to be executed correctly.

So, when you break down a process or a task, put yourself in someone else's shoes to see if the steps you outlined would make sense. If not, add the clarity and details you need to make it foolproof to get the desired results.

Hello, World

Coding requires knowing what to code, but also how to combine the tools you use together to make the project work and share with others.

Before we start getting into some heavy coding, we should work on exactly how you should use the tools together.

Create Your IntelliJ Java Project

First, we need to create the basic structure for our project. To do that, we need to go into IntelliJ and create a new Java project using specific project templates.

IntelliJ IDEA

When you launch IntelliJ for the first time, you will see the welcome screen. You can also open this screen from the **File ➤ Open** menu item.

© Doug Winnie 2021
D. Winnie, *Essential Java for AP CompSci*, https://doi.org/10.1007/978-1-4842-6183-5_8

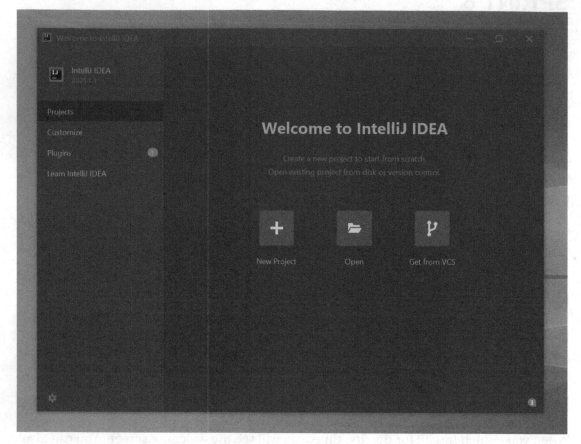

Figure 8-1. *IntelliJ welcome window*

From here, we need to create a new project, so select, you guessed it, "**Create New Project**" from the window.

You will then see the New Project window. From here, you will define the parameters for your project and set up the initial folder structure and starter code to begin coding and building your project.

First Time Only: Configure the JDK

One important component of your project is connecting it to the JDK. This isn't done automatically and needs to be done the first time you create a project and may need to be repeated each time you update the JDK on your machine.

The process is pretty simple.

At the top of the New Project window, click the "**New...**" button.

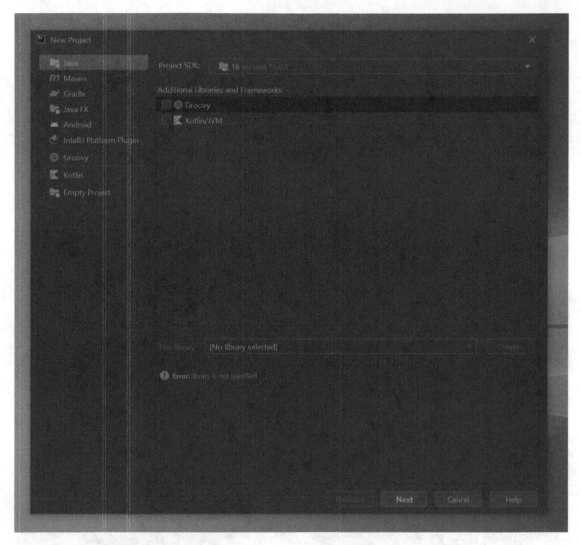

Figure 8-2. *New Project window*

When you click the "**New…**" button, you need to tell IntelliJ where the JDK is installed. On a Windows machine, it is usually located in the "**Program Files**" folder; on macOS, it is usually in the "**Library**" folder.

Select the location of the JDK and the main folder of the JDK, and then select **OK**.

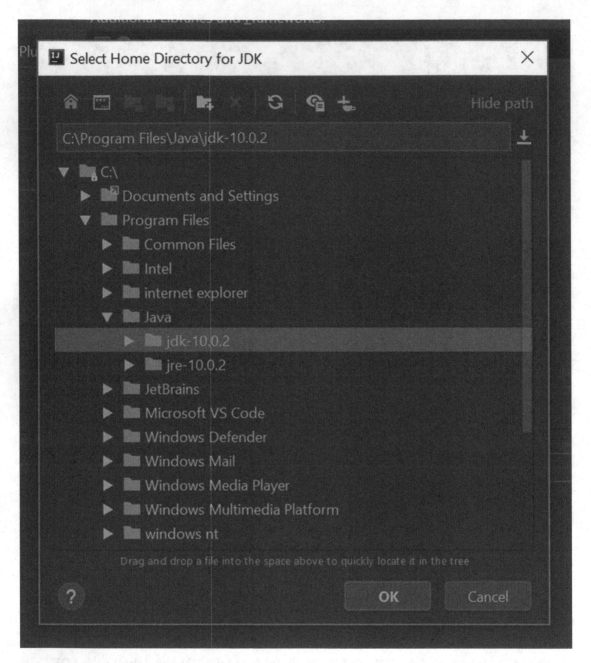

Figure 8-3. *Select the JDK folder*

You'll then see the version of the JDK appear at the top of the New Project window.

Create Project

When you have the JDK configured, get started by having Java selected on the left and keep the library and framework options unchecked.

Click **Next** to continue from the New Project window.

On the next screen, you will configure the project template.

Figure 8-4. *Project templates*

Check "Create project from template" and then select "Command Line App."

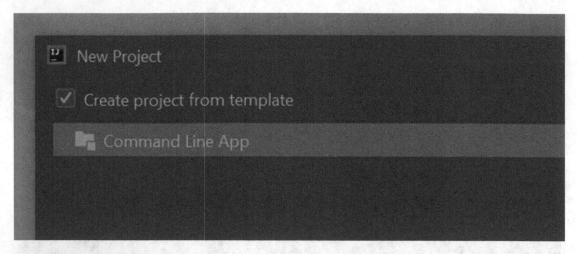

Figure 8-5. *Template selections*

Click **Next** to continue.

Now you need to give your project a name. It is highly recommended to not have any special characters or spaces in your project name. Usually for homework, you can use the name that was part of the assignment. For now, we will use "**HelloWorld**".

Then you need to select where to save your project. You can choose the default folder, and when you create the project name, it will create a subfolder for you. If you don't see it, create one under the IdeaProjects folder.

The third option is for the base package. The default package is called com.company, but we aren't going to use that so remove that and make sure the field is blank.

When you are done, you should see this:

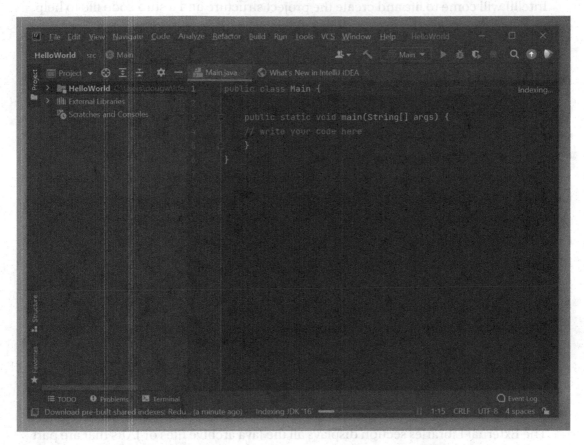

Figure 8-6. *Empty project*

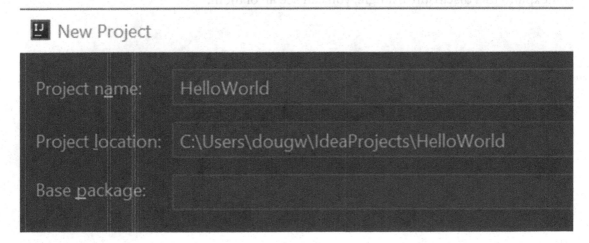

Figure 8-7. *New Project name and location*

Click **Finish** when you are ready.

IntelliJ will come to life and create the project structure and a stub code file to help you get started.

About Your Project

When the project is ready, you will see the IntelliJ interface display your main project code file, named `Main.java`. This file is where you will be building most of your project code in class assignments and homework.

On the right is the main coding area. This is where you will type your code in and you can see syntax errors and get contextual help with the features built-in to IntelliJ.

On the left is the project explorer. You can open and close this using the Alt-1 or Cmd-1 keyboard shortcuts.

The Project panel displays all the files that are in your project. The top-level folder is called the same name as the project you created. Inside, you will see a `src` folder. This contains the source code for your project. If you expand this, you will see more details of the files that are in your project, including the `Main.java` file that is already open on the right.

You will see other items here as well. The `.idea` folder contains project settings for IntelliJ that help reconfigure the IDE to your previous settings when you open the project again.

The External Libraries section displays all the Java archive files or JARs that are part of your project. Remember that the Java JDK includes all the tools for Java in JAR files. If you expand this disclosure triangle, you can see all of them.

Figure 8-8. *The Project panel*

With the initial framework of the project created, we can now write the code for our program and work with our local development environment that we have created in IntelliJ.

Coding Your Project

In IntelliJ, you will write all your project code in the code panel. Each code file is opened in a tab. Double-clicking a file in the Project panel will open it up as a new tab.

When you create a new project, you will already have a tab open for the `Main.java` file.

Writing Your First Program

I know, I know. So much talking/writing/reading, and not enough coding. Let's put that frustration to rest by writing our first program.

Now, this program isn't going to do much. But that's ok. Keep it simple for now, and we will get more complex in time. Trust me.

In your code panel, you will see a line that says:

// write your code here

Well, guess what? That's where your code goes!

Place your cursor at the end of that line of text and press Enter or Return.

Now, write the following line of code, making sure it is spelled, capitalized, and punctuated exactly as it is displayed:

```
System.out.println("Hello, World!");
```

When you are finished writing that line of code, the code panel should look like what is shown in Figure 8-9.

With the program code complete, we can now compile, build, and run the program right inside of IntelliJ.

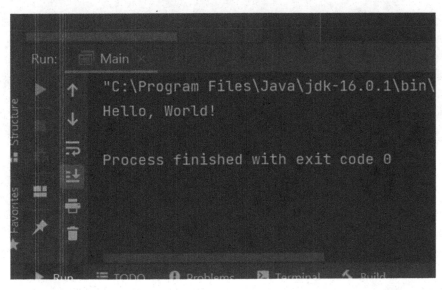

```java
public class Main {

    public static void main(String[] args) {
    // write your code here
        System.out.println("Hello, World!");
    }

}
```

Figure 8-9. *Finished Main.java file*

Compile and Run Your First Program

Open **Run ➤ Run 'Main'** from the menu. This will compile your program into Java Bytecode, building a `.class` file that will be added to your Project panel.

You will see the program begin to compile and a new panel will open at the bottom, the Run panel. This will display the results of the compilation. If there are any errors, it will list them out. In this case, there are no errors and the program runs, displaying the text "Hello, World!" on the screen.

Congrats! You have built and run your first Java program.

```
Run:    Main

    "C:\Program Files\Java\jdk-16.0.1\bin\
    Hello, World!


    Process finished with exit code 0
```

Figure 8-10. *Displaying program output*

There are some things we should look at in the Project panel however. You'll see a new folder called out. This folder contains the compiled bytecode for your project.

You will see a file called Main.class. If you remember, this file is the compiled Java bytecode that runs in the JRE. This is stored here in your project to then run on the computer. The output of the program is directed to the Run (sometimes called the Output) panel.

Now that we have a successfully running project, we should save the code to GitHub if we ever need to go back to this point later if we make changes.

Create Your Repo in GitHub

With our code saved on our local computer, we need to create a repo in GitHub for us to work with changes to our code and share it with other people.

First, open a browser and go to www.github.com. From there, we will create a new repo and upload our code.

Log in to your account, and you should see the dashboard, like the one that is shown in Figure 8-11.

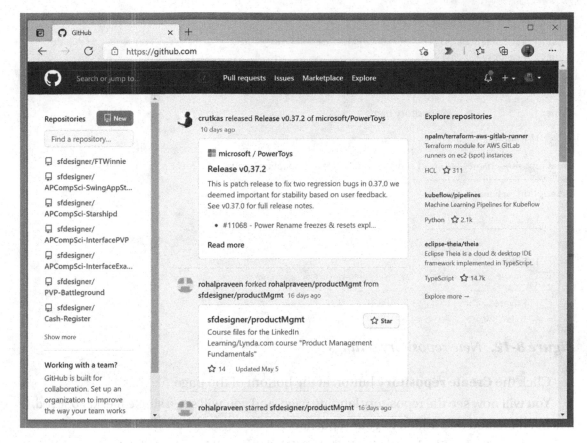

Figure 8-11. *GitHub.com dashboard*

From here, click the green **New** button on the left, or click the plus button next to your account gravatar and select **New repository**.

Give your repository a name, usually defined in the homework or assignment. For this example, we will use **HelloWorld**.

Give your repo a description, like "**First project in GitHub**."

Keep the project Public and check the **Initialize this repository with a README** option. We will be using the README to share information about our project.

You can leave all of the other options as is. Your page should look like the one in Figure 8-12.

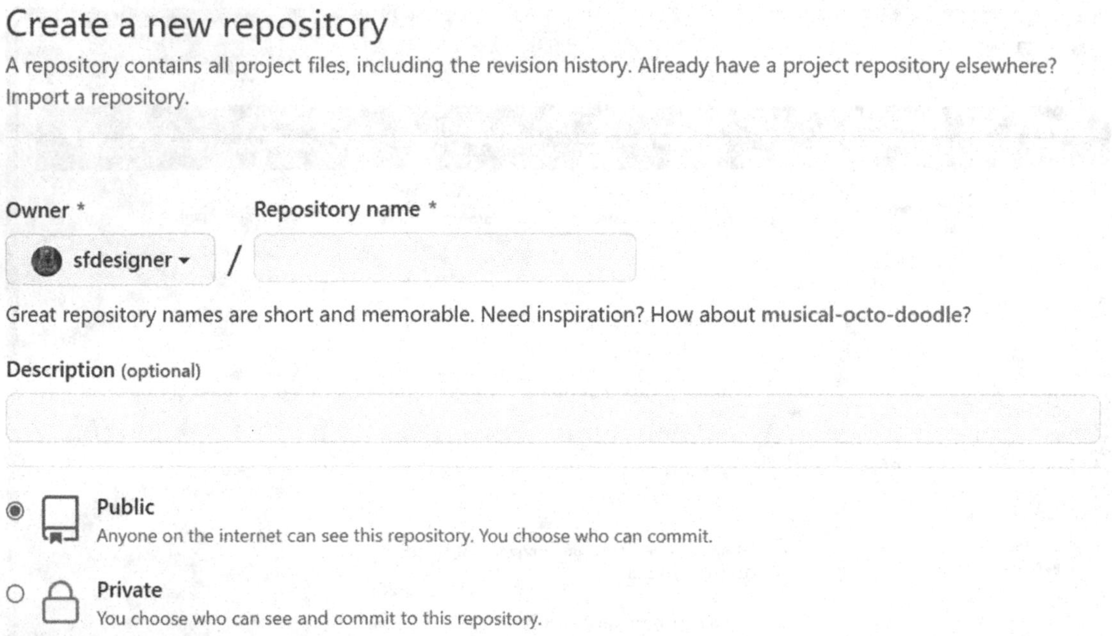

Create a new repository

A repository contains all project files, including the revision history. Already have a project repository elsewhere? Import a repository.

Owner *   **Repository name ***

[🌑 sfdesigner ▾] / [   ]

Great repository names are short and memorable. Need inspiration? How about musical-octo-doodle?

Description (optional)

[   ]

◉ 📕 **Public**
        Anyone on the internet can see this repository. You choose who can commit.

○ 🔒 **Private**
        You choose who can see and commit to this repository.

Figure 8-12. *New repository settings*

Click the **Create repository** button at the bottom of the page.

You will now see the repository landing page, and you will see a single file, README.md, has been created and added to your repository.

We can edit this file directly in GitHub. Click the pencil icon in the right side of the title bar where the README.md section starts.

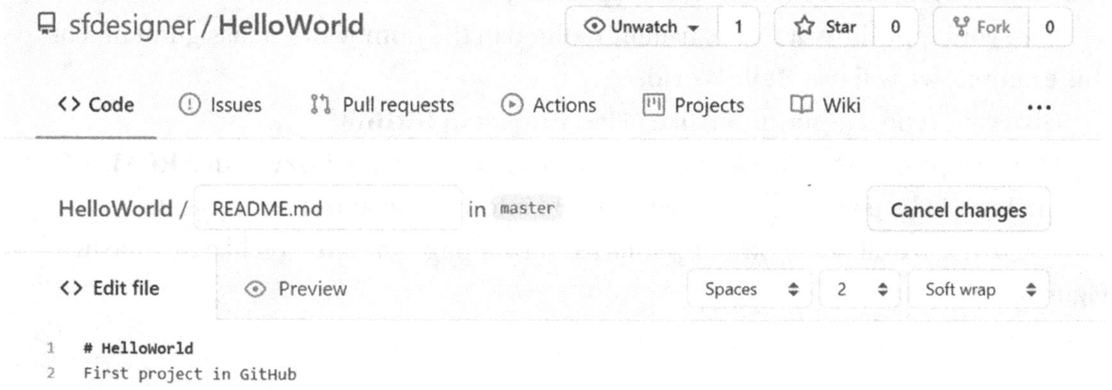

🖥 sfdesigner / **HelloWorld**   👁 Unwatch ▾ 1   ☆ Star 0   ⑂ Fork 0

⟨⟩ Code   ⊘ Issues   ⇅ Pull requests   ⊙ Actions   🗔 Projects   📖 Wiki   ···

HelloWorld /   README.md   in `master`   [**Cancel changes**]

⟨⟩ **Edit file**   ⊙ Preview   Spaces ⬍   2 ⬍   Soft wrap ⬍

```
1   # HelloWorld
2   First project in GitHub
```

Figure 8-13. *Editing README.md*

This is in a special format called Markdown. Markdown is a special language for writing formatted text. There are special extensions of the language that are specific to GitHub to help build documentation and other features for other developers to use.

I'm going to use this for my class at school, so I'll add "**Serra High School, AP CompSci**."

At the bottom, you can now save this change or commit it to the repository. Add a summary of the change, and then add an optional description like the one in Figure 8-14.

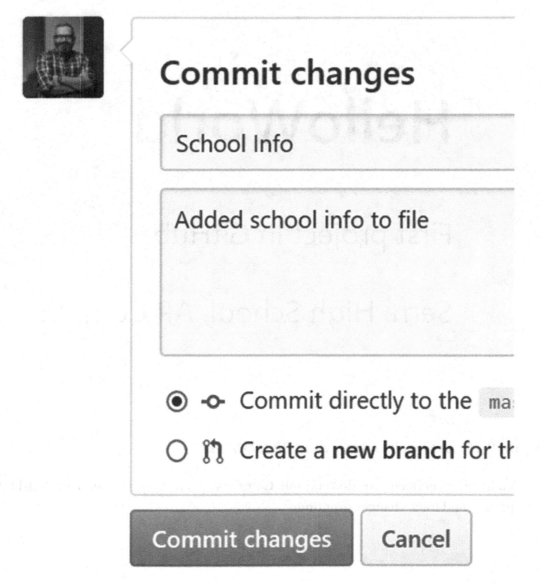

Figure 8-14. Commit change information

Then click the **Commit changes** button at the bottom.

You will now see the changes shown on the page.

```
5 lines (3 sloc) | 68 Bytes
```

HelloWorld

First project in GitHub

Serra High School, AP CompSci

Figure 8-15. *Seeing changes made to README.md*

You have just created your first commit. Commits are changes that you wish to add to your project and track changes over time.

Upload Your Code to GitHub

Now that you have your repo created, you can upload your code and keep it online to share and track changes and versions.

First, make sure you are at the main landing page for your repo. On this page, click the **Upload files** button.

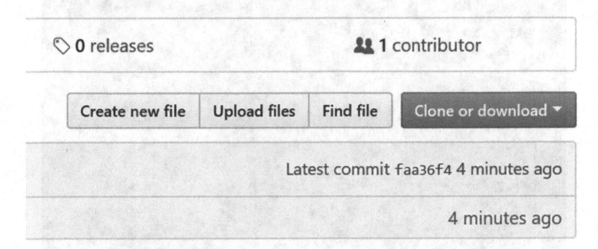

Figure 8-16. Upload files button

Now, you can drag and drop files to the area on the page, or click the **Choose your files** link and browse using the Explorer or Finder dialog box.

One trick to find your code file is to go back to IntelliJ.

From there, go to your Project panel and right-click the code file you want to upload. Select the **Show in Explorer** or **Show in Finder** option.

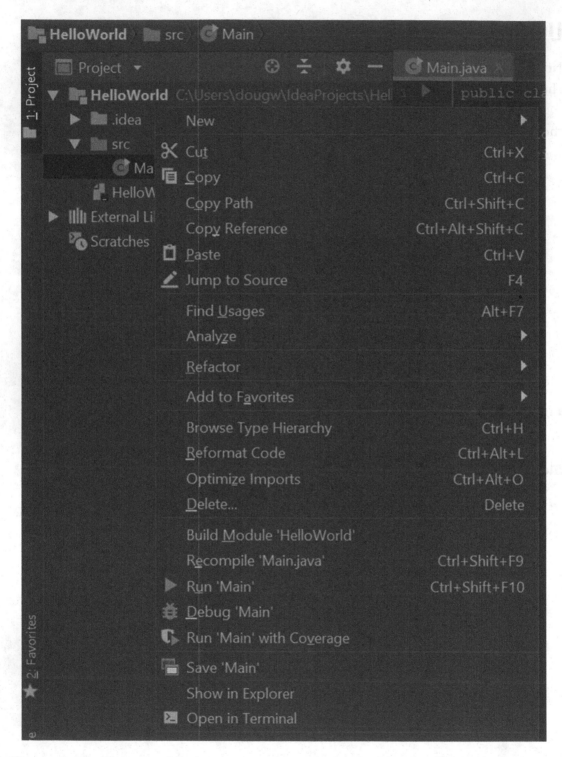

Figure 8-17. *Show in... option*

That will then open a window and display the file. You can now drag and drop that into GitHub in the browser.

You will see the file added to the bottom of the file drop target zone.

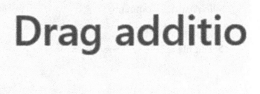

 Main.java

Figure 8-18. *File ready to commit*

Now, we can commit our changes. For the summary, put "**First code commit**" and then for the extended description "**Display a statement on the screen.**"

Click the green **Commit changes** button when you are finished.

GitHub will then process your changes and then display them in the repository window.

Sharing Program Output

When you are using the exercises in this book and are collaborating with others, it might be helpful to share the output of your program as well. To do that, we will create a text file and copy and paste the contents from the Run panel into the text file.

To start, create a new file in your repo; call it output.txt.

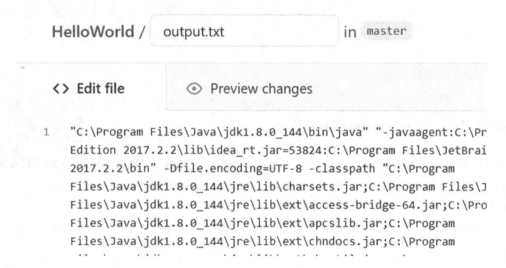

Figure 8-19. *Creating a text file*

From IntelliJ, go to your HelloWorld project and click inside the Run panel. If the panel isn't open, run the program again to display it.

Press Control-A or Command-A to select all, and then copy to the clipboard. Then go back to the new text file in GitHub and paste.

HelloWorld / output.txt   in master

<> **Edit file**   ⊙ **Preview changes**

```
1   "C:\Program Files\Java\jdk1.8.0_144\bin\java" "-javaagent:C:\Pr
    Edition 2017.2.2\lib\idea_rt.jar=53824:C:\Program Files\JetBrai
    2017.2.2\bin" -Dfile.encoding=UTF-8 -classpath "C:\Program
    Files\Java\jdk1.8.0_144\jre\lib\charsets.jar;C:\Program Files\J
    Files\Java\jdk1.8.0_144\jre\lib\ext\access-bridge-64.jar;C:\Pro
    Files\Java\jdk1.8.0_144\jre\lib\ext\apcslib.jar;C:\Program
    Files\Java\jdk1.8.0_144\jre\lib\ext\chndocs.jar;C:\Program
```

Figure 8-20. *Pasted output text*

Go to the bottom of the page and click the **Commit new file** button.

Simple Java Program Structure

In our first program, we displayed a single message on the computer. We did this using the System.out.println() method. This is a command in Java that we can use to perform certain actions.

Well, actually, println() is the method really. System.out is the class that contains the println() method we run. And every statement in Java ends with a semicolon. Every. One. It is like the period for a sentence.

You see, almost everything in Java is saved in something called a class. A class defines the rules for how parts of our program work. Later, you will learn how to work with classes more and even how to make your own. For now, we will need to just work with the ones that we already have available to us.

When we run our code from before

```
System.out.println("Hello, world!");
```

there are a few things that are going on.

First, everything around this line of code sets up our project in Java. Let's look at it briefly.

Listing 9-1. Basic program structure

```
public class Main {

    public static void main(String[] args) {
        System.out.println("Hello, World");
    }
}
```

© Doug Winnie 2021
D. Winnie, *Essential Java for AP CompSci*, https://doi.org/10.1007/978-1-4842-6183-5_9

In this example code, our `Hello, World` statement is within two specific code blocks. A code block is defined using a pair of curly braces, or { }. These group the contents within them into a block.

Blocks have some rules around them, but we'll cover those later. For now, just know that you can take blocks and put them inside of one another. So, in this example, we have a `public class Main` code block that starts on line 1 and ends on 6. We then have `public static void main` code block that starts on 3 and ends on 5.

Our code is within this inner code block.

The outer block defines the overall wrapper for our program. Java looks for a `main()` method to execute when it builds and runs the program.

So, Java looks for a class. It finds it.

Then it looks for the `main()` method, which it also finds.

Then it runs the code within the method. That's the code we created and added to the project.

Until we get to object-oriented programming, all of your code will be in the Main.java file. Soon, we will also create code outside of the constructor.

Those `public`, `class`, `static`, `void` phrases? Just ignore them for now and focus on what we put into the `main()` method. Everything will make sense in time.

Text Literals and Output

Computers take things literally. Like, literally. So much that there are things actually called literals.

Literally.

"Hello, World" is a literal. A text literal to be precise.

A text literal contains letters, symbols, punctuation, and numbers and is denoted by a pair of quotation marks. The double quotes mark the beginning and the end of the literal.

Text Output

When you run a method like `println()`, it is looking for something called a string. A string is another word for text. Think of it like a sequence of letter beads on a string.

When you provide a string to a method that uses a string, it will do something with it. In the case of `println()`, it will print it to the screen and then move to the next line.

So, if you have the following statements:

```
System.out.println("Hello");
System.out.println("World");
```

this would output as

```
Hello
World
```

Displaying both on two lines.

But there is another method you can use, `print()`. This works the same way, but you don't move to the next line after the text displays.

© Doug Winnie 2021
D. Winnie, *Essential Java for AP CompSci*, https://doi.org/10.1007/978-1-4842-6183-5_10

So, if you have these statements:

```
System.out.print("Hello");
System.out.print("World");
```

this would output as

```
HelloWorld
```

Putting both characters on the same line.

Escape Sequences

Text literals can contain special characters as well. Take the previous example:

```
System.out.print("Hello");
System.out.print("World");
```

If you wanted to include a new line in the text literal itself, you can add it using the two-letter sequence \n.

This is called the newline character. And it will create a line break in your text:

```
System.out.print("Hello\n");
System.out.print("World");
```

It is essentially the same as

```
System.out.print("Hello\nWorld");
```

And it displays this on the screen:

```
Hello
World
```

How about this one?

If you wanted to display the following line, how would you do it?

```
Mike said, "Hey!"
```

This line of text has a quote in it, so if we created a text literal with it, we would have

```
"Mike said, "Hey!""
```

But the computer, again, is dumb. So, it will think that the quote before the H in Hey is the end of the literal.

Not what we wanted.

To get around this, we can use an escape sequence to tell the program that the quotes around Hey are part of the literal, not the boundaries of it:

```
"Mike said, \"Hey\""
```

Now the slash quote two-character sequence can allow the literal to include the quote.

There are others you can use too, including the tab space sequence.

The tab sequence, \t, adds a tab space in your text. This is sometimes helpful to align things into columns if you get the right sequence setup.

Like this one:

```
"First\tMiddle\tLast"
"R.\tDouglas\tWinnie"
```

This would display as

```
First       Middle       Last
R.          Douglas      Winnie
```

The tab space shifts over to help line things up when you stack statements on top of one another.

Value Literals

Computers store, process, and access data and information. In a computer program, a programmer does this with variables. Variables have two sides to them. For the programmer, it is a name that you use to refer to a value throughout your program. The computer then reserves an amount of space in memory to store that value and make it available to you as a programmer.

The easiest value to think of is a number. Like the number three. Three is a number of things, like three paperclips. The number three is called an integer. An integer is a whole number that counts the number of objects or things. With an integer, I can add to it or subtract from it.

There are two types of integers however: unsigned and signed. When you think of three paperclips, you don't think in terms of positive or negative. You just simply have three paperclips. But if I used to have five paperclips and now have three, how would I represent the change in value? I would use a negative number to indicate that I have a difference of –2.

Negative numbers can be plotted on a number line along with other numbers that can be either positive or negative. To represent these values, you need a sign before them to show positive or negative value. Even though the positive sign is assumed most of the time, in a signed number it is still there. This sign needs to be saved by the computer, so space needs to be reserved for it.

If we were selling the paperclips, we would need to represent the price. Currency is measured as a decimal, or fractions of a whole number. So, the paperclip could be $0.25 or €0,25 or £0.25. Decimals might be less than one, but the details of the fraction need to be captured in data in some form. It doesn't matter to the computer if a number is a million or a millionth. It all needs to store the details of the value the same way in memory.

© Doug Winnie 2021
D. Winnie, *Essential Java for AP CompSci*, https://doi.org/10.1007/978-1-4842-6183-5_11

Literal Formatting

While we can look at these numbers and tell the difference, the computer—you guessed it—is dumb. It can't tell the difference between number formats unless to specifically tell it what they are.

Literals are source code representation of a fixed value. They are represented directly in code without any computation.

The format we provide these values defines their types.

We already encountered a string literal. It is defined by characters that are placed within a set of quotation marks.

There is another related letter type, called a character. It is simply a single character wrapped in single quotes:

Character: `'A'`, `'g'`, `'&'`

String literals: `"Hello, world"`, `"Mr. Winnie"`, `"47"`

The escape sequences we learned are converted to individual characters that perform unique output operations like tab spaces, line returns, and others. So we can add these to string literals:

Strings containing quotes:

`"Janet said, \"Hello!\""`

Strings containing new lines:

`"Line one\nLine two"`

For numbers, things are a bit different. There are two basic types of numbers: integers and decimals.

Integers are whole numbers and can never hold any fractional value less than one. Decimals can hold fractions of a whole number. Typically, we represent these as either a number without a decimal point or a number with one:

Integer: `23`, `55`, `1701`

Decimal: `23.0`, `3.14`, `47.001`

There are two types of decimal numbers though. (Nothing is easy with computers, is it?) And it all comes down to memory.

Imagine you have a decimal number that measures the distance between two chairs. Probably, you could measure that in whole numbers, like 15 inches.

Imagine if you needed to measure the distance between two wires on a circuit board. You would need a lot more precision there, probably 0.0005 inches.

Now, what if you needed to measure the distance between two atoms in a molecule? Take carbon monoxide. The distance between a carbon atom and an oxygen atom is 1.13×10^{10} m or .000000000113 m. That is going to require a lot more precision to be accurate.

Precision is the mirror of quantity. The more of something you have, the more memory you need. In that same vein, the more precise you need to be, the more memory you need.

But sometimes, you don't need the precision right away. So how do we represent that as a value literal?

We add suffixes to the numbers.

There are two basic precisions for decimal numbers: float and double. To tell the difference between them, you add a suffix at the end. For float, you add an f. For double, you add a d:

Float decimal number literals: `65.4f`

Double number literals: `65.4d`

This will allow these literals to be managed with different levels of precision. Typically, you won't need to worry about these for most applications, unless you work in the medical or scientific fields. In addition, a number that is missing a suffix is considered a double number.

Output Formatting

What a value is and how we display it are two different things. We can adapt how we display various value literals through formatters that convert and display values in different ways.

To do this, we will use the `printf()` method that will contain the information we want to display, but includes special codes that change the way the values are shown on the screen.

Decimal Formatters

The most basic is when we work with decimals. Sometimes, we need to display more digits in a number than are needed.

Here's the code for how this works.

Listing 12-1. Decimal formatters

```
System.out.println(2.3f);
System.out.printf("%.2f",2.3f);
System.out.println();
System.out.printf("%.4f",2.3f);
System.out.println();
```

Here's how it works. You start with the `println()` statement, and then you create a string literal that holds the text you want to display.

Then, you use the percent sign to create a marker in the literal. Immediately following, you add the formatting code.

After the formatter string literal, you follow with a comma and the value you want to insert into the first place. You can insert more than one value in a string formatter, just separate them with commas.

© Doug Winnie 2021
D. Winnie, *Essential Java for AP CompSci*, https://doi.org/10.1007/978-1-4842-6183-5_12

The example in Listing 12-1 outputs the following:

```
2.3
2.30
2.3000
```

The %.2f code means that we are providing a floating-point number (a number with a decimal) with two digits in the decimal. This is defined using the f character in the code.

The last example uses %.4f that provides four digits in the output.

Thousands Formatters

For a larger number, it is easier to read it if you use commas to separate each level of thousand in the number (or a period if you are in other parts of the world).

To do that, you add a comma in the formatter code. Also, if you are working with integers, or numbers without fractions, you use the character d in the formatter instead of f.

Listing 12-2. Thousands formatter

```
System.out.println(1000000);
System.out.printf("%,d",1000000);
System.out.println();
```

The output in this example is

```
1000000
1,000,000
```

Currency Formatters

We can combine other text in with the formatter string and combine multiple formatters together. For example, what if we wanted to show a price? We should show that with two decimal places and with a thousands separator in the number.

Listing 12-3. Currency formatter

```
System.out.println(1000.2f);
System.out.printf("$%.2f", 1000.2f);
System.out.println();
System.out.printf("$%,.2f", 1000.2f);
System.out.println();
```

We are combining multiple formatters here, but we are also prefixing the formatter with a dollar sign. You can add your formatter codes in any string literal when you use the printf() statement.

This example outputs the following:

```
1000.2
$1000.20
$1,000.20
```

Spacing and Alignment Formatters

Often for text, you want to align or create a fixed amount of space for certain values or strings. You can use a string formatter to do exactly that by using the character s in your formatter code.

Check out this example.

Listing 12-4. Spacing and alignment formatters

```
System.out.println("Hello!");
System.out.printf("|%20s|", "Hello!");
System.out.println();
System.out.printf("|%-20s|", "Hello!");
System.out.println();
System.out.printf("|%-20s|", "Hello, this is a long sentence.!");
System.out.println();
System.out.printf("|%-20.20s|", "Hello, this is a long sentence.!");
System.out.println();
```

The output for this is

```
Hello!
|              Hello!|
|Hello!              |
|Hello, this is a long sentence.!|
|Hello, this is a lon|
```

The pipes (the vertical lines) are added to make it clearer on what is going on here.

When you use a string formatter, the whole number value represents the minimum amount of characters the phrase is allowed to take up on the screen. So %20s will take up 20 characters of space on the screen.

If you add a minus sign to it, it will adjust the alignment, so it is on the other side. In this case, left aligned.

If you have a long string, it will print it out in its entirety, unless you add a decimal portion to the formatter. In this case, it will cut off any text that is longer than the maximum string length allowed by the formatter.

Multiple Items in Formatters

You can add as many codes in your formatter string as you want; you just need to make sure you have a matching value to place inside of it. Each of these values is separated by commas.

Listing 12-5. Multiple items in a formatter

```
System.out.printf("%10s $%.2f\n","Apples",1.4f);
System.out.printf("%10s $%.2f\n","Brownies",0.8f);
```

The output for this one is

```
    Apples $1.40
  Brownies $0.80
```

Again, you can insert as many formatting codes as you want, but each value needs to be separated by a comma after it.

Listing 12-6. Sprint 12 code

```java
public class Main {

    public static void main(String[] args) {
        /* String Formatting */

        // Display a decimal number
        System.out.println(2.3f);
        System.out.printf("%.2f",2.3f);
        System.out.println();
        System.out.printf("%.4f",2.3f);
        System.out.println();
        /* Output
        2.3
        2.30
        2.3000
         */

        // Display a thousands separator
        System.out.println(1000000);
        System.out.printf("%,d",1000000);
        System.out.println();
        /* Output
        1000000
        1,000,000
         */

        // Display a price
        System.out.println(1000.2f);
        System.out.printf("$%.2f", 1000.2f);
        System.out.println();
        System.out.printf("$%,.2f", 1000.2f);
        System.out.println();
```

```java
/* Output:
1000.2
$1000.20
$1,000.20
 */

// Display a string
System.out.println("Hello!");
System.out.printf("|%20s|", "Hello!");
System.out.println();
System.out.printf("|%-20s|", "Hello!");
System.out.println();
System.out.printf("|%-20s|", "Hello, this is a long sentence.!");
System.out.println();
System.out.printf("|%-20.20s|", "Hello, this is a long sentence.!");
System.out.println();
/* Output:
Hello!
|              Hello!|
|Hello!              |
|Hello, this is a long sentence.!|
|Hello, this is a lon|
 */

// Display multiple items in a single string
System.out.printf("%10s $%.2f\n","Apples",1.4f);
System.out.printf("%10s $%.2f\n","Brownies",0.8f);
/* Output
    Apples $1.40
  Brownies $0.80
 */
    }
}
```

Comments and Whitespace

Psst.

Wanna make a comment on something?

It's pretty easy.

Start it with a double slash, //, and anything after that is ignored by the compiler, and you can write whatever you want.

Oh?

You want to say more?

Well, then start your novel with a slash asterisk, /*, and then end it with an asterisk slash, */.

Listing 13-1. Single-line and multiline comments

```
// Single line comment

/* Multi-line
   comment
*/
```

Oh, and wanna know a cool trick?

If you put a comment before a line of code or wrap it as a multiline comment, you will prevent the program from seeing the code.

That's called commenting out your code.

Ooooh! And one more thing. There is a shortcut in IntelliJ to do that. Just select the code you want to comment out and press Control-/ or Command-/.

Neat, right?

© Doug Winnie 2021
D. Winnie, *Essential Java for AP CompSci*, https://doi.org/10.1007/978-1-4842-6183-5_13

Abstraction of Numbers

When we think about numbers, we think of, well, numbers. Anything that has a digit that could be zero through nine. So, for example, we have a number like 723. This number 723 represents a value, or a count of something. It could be 723 dollars, 723 yards of yarn, or 723 gallons of milk. The number tells you how much of something there is.

But what if I showed you these three numbers? 723, 723, and 723. What if I told you that each of these numbers actually represented different amounts of something? It is totally possible, through the use of different number systems.

Let's throw away numbers as we know them for a moment and look at a pile of stuff. In this case, I have five paperclips. Now we can represent this as a five, but if I said I have V paperclips, does that mean the same thing? Yep. It does if you understand Roman numerals. Roman numerals are another way to represent how much of something we have. It follows a different set of rules using symbols like I, V, X, L, C, and M. Roman numerals are based on basic counting. Starting at one, I add symbols, and then at a certain point, I use the next largest symbol and either add or subtract from that value with the understanding that there can only be three consecutive symbols of the same type.

Confusing? Kinda. But for centuries, Roman numerals have been used as the basic form for all representations of value back in Roman days, to counting annual sporting events, or movie sequels today. But this shows that there can be more than one way to represent the same value.

We ordinarily represent numbers using decimal numbers. Decimal uses a base of 10 for the number system. Which is why there are ten digits that we use for numbers: 0, 1, 2, 3, 4, 5, 6, 7, 8, and 9. The other key part of a number system is the fact that you can have multiple digits. So, for example, we take the number 5, and we can represent that as a single digit. But the number 15 we need two digits. The digit on the right represents "ones"; the next digit to the left represents "tens."

© Doug Winnie 2021
D. Winnie, *Essential Java for AP CompSci*, https://doi.org/10.1007/978-1-4842-6183-5_14

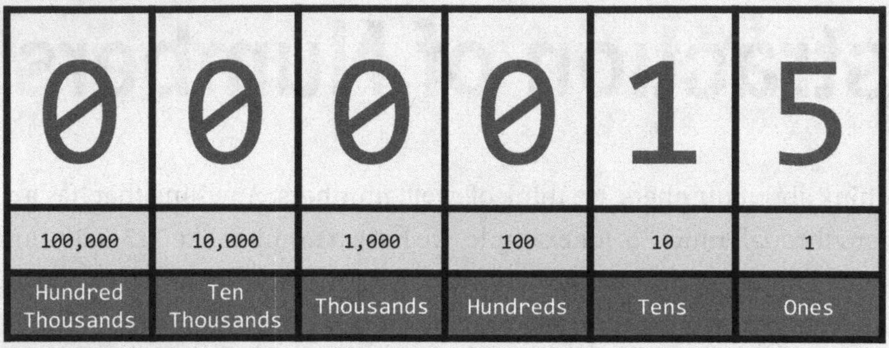

0	0	0	0	1	5
100,000	10,000	1,000	100	10	1
Hundred Thousands	Ten Thousands	Thousands	Hundreds	Tens	Ones

Figure 14-1. *Numerical digits*

We can represent this like an old-style odometer, where all of the possible digits can be shown in a column. When you get to the highest digit and need to add one more, you push the value to the next column and start over from zero.

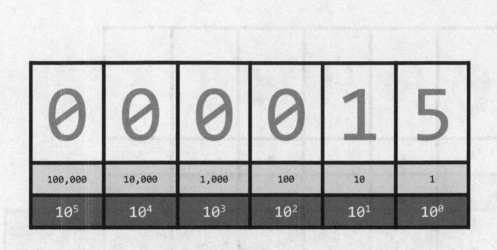

Figure 14-2. *Decimal digits as powers of 10*

There is some cool math that goes with these columns. Remember when I said that decimal is based on 10? Well, you can represent the first column as taking its single digit and multiplying it by 10 to the power of 0, which is 1. As you move to the left, you can take the exponent and increase it by one for as long as you need to. So the next column is 10 to the power of 1 which is 10, multiplied by the digit in the column.

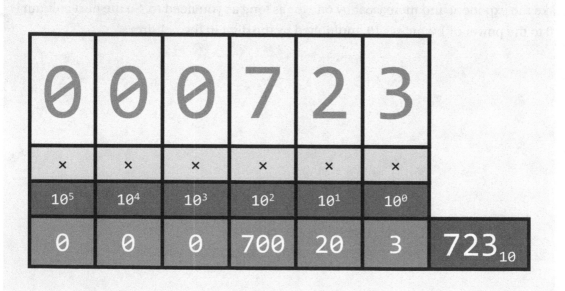

Figure 14-3. *15 in power of tens*

So if we take a more complicated example like our earlier 723, we can calculate what each column represents, and when you add all of these up, you come back to 723.

Figure 14-4. *723 in powers of tens*

But what if I took the number of possible digits and cut off the last two? In this case, we would have only eight digits, creating a new number system based on eight, or the octal number system.

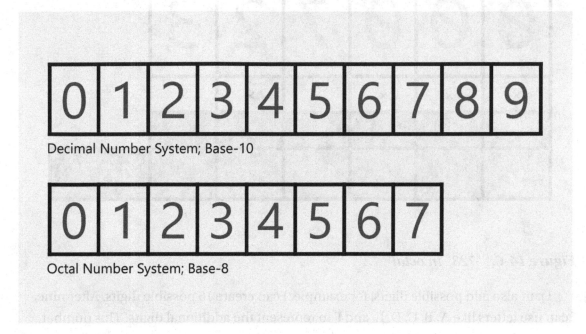

Decimal Number System; Base-10

Octal Number System; Base-8

Figure 14-5. *Decimal vs. octal*

I now need to change the calculations for the columns, and instead of using ten, I need to use eight. So now if I use the same format to calculate each column, the octal number of 723 actually is 467 in decimal.

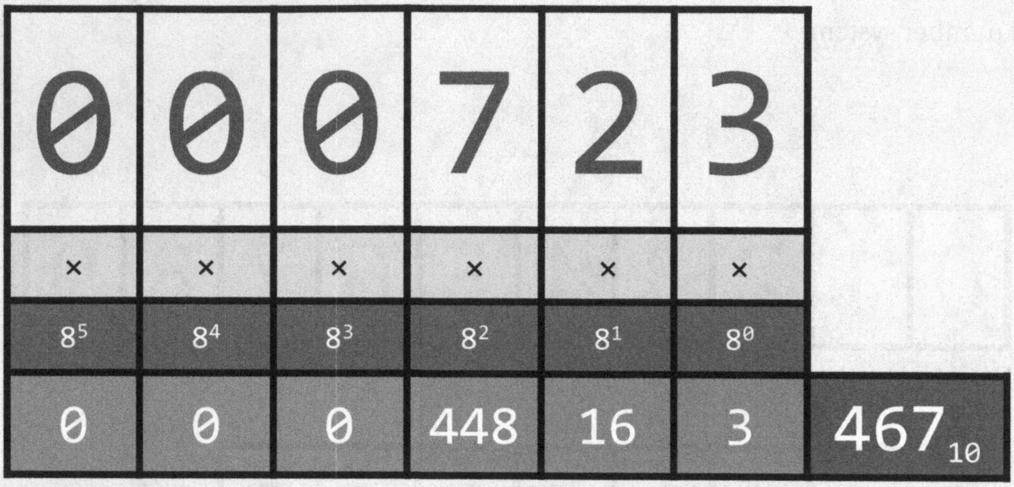

0	0	0	7	2	3	
×	×	×	×	×	×	
8^5	8^4	8^3	8^2	8^1	8^0	
0	0	0	448	16	3	467_{10}

Figure 14-6. *"723" in octal*

I can also add possible digits, for example, I can create 16 possible digits. After nine, I can use letters like A, B, C, D, E, and F to represent the additional digits. This number system is based on 16 and is called the hexadecimal system.

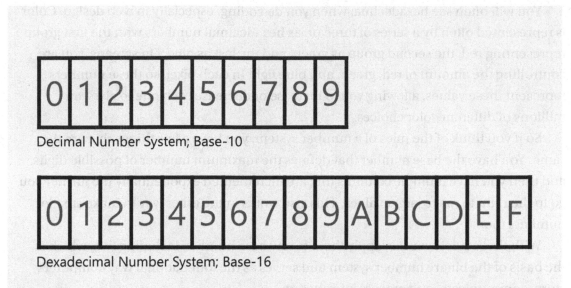

Figure 14-7. *Decimal vs. hexadecimal*

So 723 in hexadecimal, when we update our formulas for the columns of the digits, actually represents what we would recognize as 1827 in decimal.

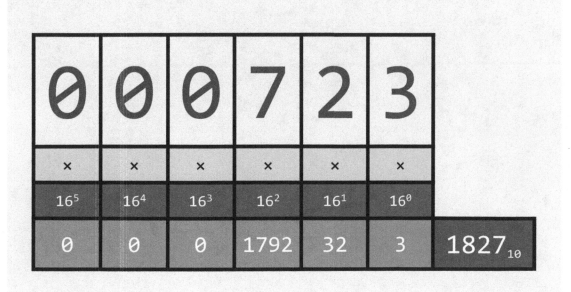

Figure 14-8. *"723" in hexadecimal*

You will often see hexadecimal when you do coding, especially in web design. Color is represented often by a series of three or six hexadecimal numbers with the first group representing red, the second group as green, and the last as blue. On screens, you are controlling the amount of red, green, and blue light in each pixel, so these numbers represent these values, allowing you to increase or decrease each one to give you millions of different color choices.

So if you think of the rules of a number system, you have a few things that are the same. You have the base number that defines the maximum number of possible digits, and then you have multiple columns that are incremented exponentially the further you go to the right to make larger values. This also works in the other way to make smaller numbers too.

With those rules, you can apply them to any base number, including two, which is the basis of the binary number system and serves as the foundational way computers store, communicate, and process information.

Binary

We can represent the binary states of "on" and "off" as numbers. The binary number system is based on only two digits: one and zero. For a binary state of on, that's represented by a one. For a binary state of off, that's represented by a zero.

But storing a single value doesn't make much sense on its own. You would want to store multiple values in a row. To do that, you would create a string of them, and since they are all numbers, you are just creating a larger number with multiple digits or bits.

A grouping of eight binary digits is called a byte, spelled with a y. A byte is a common measure of data that we use every day. A kilobyte is 1024 bytes. A megabyte is 1024 kilobytes. A gigabyte is 1024 megabytes, and a terabyte is 1024 gigabytes.

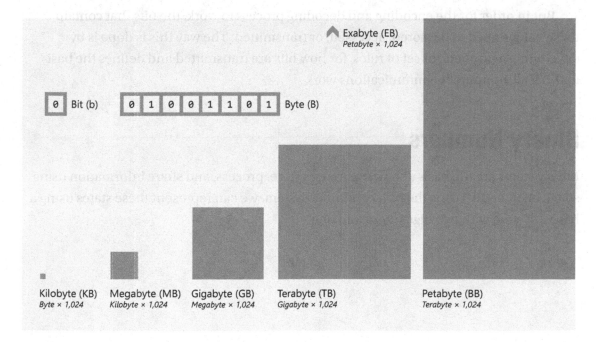

Figure 15-1. *Memory and storage sizes*

© Doug Winnie 2021

D. Winnie, *Essential Java for AP CompSci*, https://doi.org/10.1007/978-1-4842-6183-5_15

On a computer, you might have a drive that can store a terabyte of data. A terabyte can contain almost nine trillion bits. That's over nine trillion individual states of on or off.

But what do we do with all of these bits?

Each of these bits holds an on or off state that represents a tiny part of a larger piece of information, whether it is a single number, a piece of text called a string, a document, a photo, a song, a movie, or a computer program. All of these things we work with every day are translated to bits that are stored, transmitted, and translated by computers and networks.

The process of taking information that we recognize today, like a string of text, and converting it to binary is called encoding. You are taking something that we represent in a way humans can understand it and are finding a way to convert it using a specific process into a string of binary digits that can be transmitted, processed, and stored by a computer or network.

Using that same process, but in reverse, those individual binary digits can be converted back to the information we work with every day. This is called decoding. It reconstitutes the files that are transmitted or accessed and presents them to us in a format we can recognize.

But in order for the encoding and decoding process to work, the bits that contain these values need to be stored, accessed, or transmitted. The way this is done is by developing a protocol, or set of rules, for how bits are transmitted and defines the basis for how all computer communications work.

Binary Numbers

Binary states are the basis of how computers store, process, and share information using states of on or off. Using the binary number system, we can represent these states using a base 2 system with two digits: zero and one.

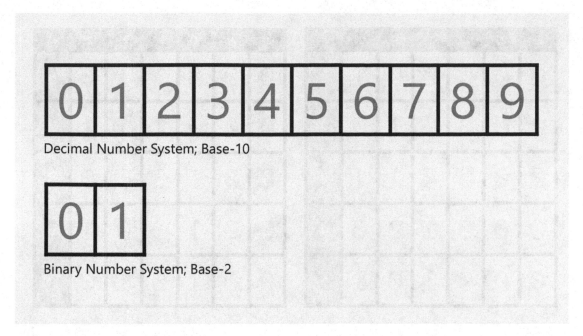

Figure 15-2. Decimal vs. binary

Using the rules of number systems, we can create a system for what a binary digit looks like. We have a maximum of two possible digits: zero and one. We then also have multiple columns that exponentially increase in value from right to left based on two, the base number of the system. If we count up from zero, we can see how binary begins to work. First, I start with zero, then I add one, making it one. If I add another one, I have maxed out the possible number of digits in the first column, so I then carry that over to the next column, and return back to zero in the first.

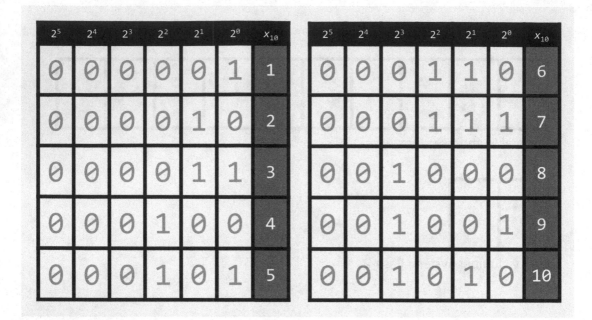

Figure 15-3. *Counting to "10" in binary*

We continue to add one, adding digits to the number, and eventually get one that is several digits consisting of multiple ones and zeros. Using the formula we can apply to each column, we can take each column and multiply the digit by the base number raised to the power of the column. Let's walk through that column by column.

Figure 15-4. *Converting binary to decimal*

We have the number 10011. Starting from the right, we take the column which is 2 to the 0 power which is 1 and multiply it by the digit, which makes 1.

The next column is 2 to the 1st power, which is 2; multiply it by 1 which is 2.

Next we have 2 to the 2nd power, which is 4, times 0 is 0.

Next is 2 to the 3rd power, which is 8, times 0 is 0.

And last, we have 2 to the 4th power, which is 16, times 1 is 16.

Then we add all of those together: 16, plus 0, plus 0, plus 2, plus 1, totaling 19.

We can also do this in the other direction. Let's take the number 23.

0	23−16	7<8	7−4	3−2	1−1	
0	1	0	1	1	1	
×	×	×	×	×	×	
2^5	2^4	2^3	2^2	2^1	2^0	
0	16	0	4	2	1	23_{10}

Figure 15-5. *Converting decimal to binary*

We can use the formulas for the binary digit columns to convert the decimal number to binary.

We would need to find the largest power of 2 that is less than 23, which is 16. We would then put a 1 in that column and subtract 16 from 23, leaving 7.

The next column is 2 to the power of 4, or 8. The number we are carrying over is too small, so we put a 0 and move on.

The largest power of 2 in 7 is 4, so we put a 1 in that column and subtract from 7, leaving 3.

The next largest power in 3 is 2, so we put a 1 in that column and subtract from 3, leaving 1, which is equal to the next largest power which is 1. The result is 10111.

So using this algorithm, a computer can take a value that we would represent as a decimal number and can convert it into a format that can be natively stored and transmitted, using ones and zeros. This conversion process is the basis of all encoding and decoding of digital information we work with every day.

Bit Size and Values

With binary numbers, we can store values that we would ordinarily represent in decimal in a format that the computer can store and send or receive. But as we think about values, the more digits that are in a number, the larger the value can be.

Let's take this binary number: 10. This is a two-bit digit, meaning that it contains two digits, each one being a bit, a one or a zero. This two-bit number can store four different values and has a maximum value of three. As we add additional digits, we increase the maximum value we can store in that binary number.

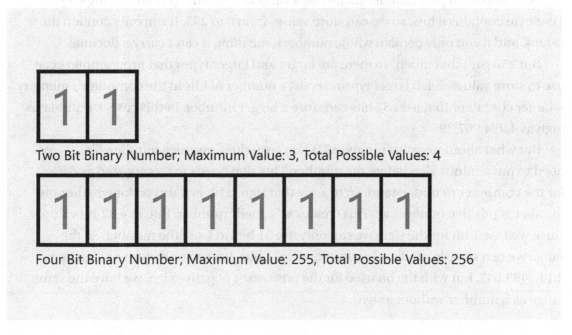

Two Bit Binary Number; Maximum Value: 3, Total Possible Values: 4

Four Bit Binary Number; Maximum Value: 255, Total Possible Values: 256

Figure 15-6. *Binary number bit sizes*

Have you heard the term 8-bit? 8-bit, 16-bit, 32-bit, 64-bit, and higher, these are all representations of the number of digits that are available to store in a binary number. If we look at an 8-bit number, we have eight columns or eight possible digits. If we do the math for each column, we can store a maximum value of 255. If we add 0 which is a value of nothing, we can store a total of 256 values, from 0 to 255. And what is 2 to the 8th power? It's 256.

But 256 is not a very high number. So if we need to store a larger number, we need more bits. If we add more to make a 16-bit number, we can store up to a value of 65,535 or 65,536 values including 0.

Need more? Let's double it to 32-bit. Now we can store 4,294,967,296 values.

64-bit can store over 18 quintillion values, and the number gets larger and larger the more bits we add.

Using these bits, a computer program can store values in memory. A programmer needs to balance the storage requirements of their applications to the amount that is available for the program. To help manage that, developers have different sizes and types of containers, called variables, that they can use to store information. Each variable type has different bit size requirements, meaning that the variable has a limited size that the programmer can store values into.

For example, a programmer might use a variable type that requires a single byte. That byte contains 8 bits, so we can store values from 0 to 255. It can only contain those values, and it can only contain whole numbers, meaning it can't carry a decimal.

But 255 isn't that much, so there are larger and larger types that programmers can use to store values. Each larger type reserves a number of bits in the computer's memory. A larger container that uses 32 bits can store a bigger number. In this case, a number as high as 4,294,967,295.

But what about negative numbers? When we write a negative number, like –5, we need to put a minus sign before the number. This sign needs to be captured as data for the computer to understand. So to store that sign, a bit is reserved for whether the number is positive or negative. This creates a "signed" number. But, in a 32-bit value, since we lose 1 bit for the sign, we can only use 31 bits to store the number. So the range we can store is smaller. As a result, with 31 bits, we can only store a value up to 2,147,483,647, but with the bit used for the positive or negative sign, we have the same range as a number without a sign.

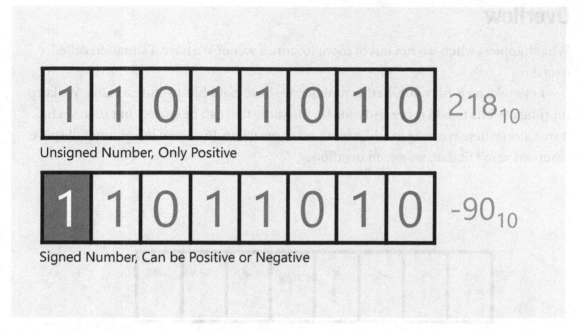

Figure 15-7. Unsigned and signed numbers

A programmer can easily store one or a few of these values without worrying about numbers. But what about something like a spreadsheet? Let's assume a single cell can store a value using 64 bits. That's a number that can hold a lot of information and can easily store positive, negative, and even decimal numbers for us to do calculations with. 64 bits is equal to 8 bytes. So that seems harmless enough.

But a spreadsheet can contain tons of data in it. In fact, Excel spreadsheets can contain 1,048,576 rows and 16,384 columns. That's 17,179,869,184 cells of data! With each one requiring 8 bytes, that's 137,438,953,472 bytes or 128 gigabytes of storage. Yikes! Luckily, programmers and computers have ways to compress and reduce the amount of space that files like spreadsheets have to take. But you can see how you can quickly take up a lot of room.

So while it might seem like a computer can handle all the data you can throw at it, it isn't quite that simple. When a developer has to limit themselves to the available memory on a phone, which could have only one or two gigabytes of memory, with a lot of that already used by the operating system, a lot of care needs to be taken in how to use the memory that is available and to avoid slowing down the system by taking up too much space.

Overflow

What happens when we run out of room to store a value? We have a situation called overflow.

Let's take an 8-bit value. In this number, we have eight bits to store a value. We keep flipping the bits to add more and more to the value that can be stored, but then we hit a situation where we have to add a ninth bit to the value. But since the amount of space reserved won't fit that, we get an overflow.

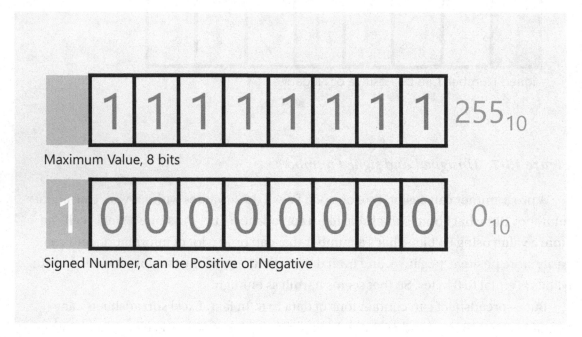

Maximum Value, 8 bits

Signed Number, Can be Positive or Negative

Figure 15-8. *Adding 1 to a maximum value*

Some overflows happen, and you get an error. Like when you take a calculator and try to get a number larger than the digits that can be displayed on the screen. But sometimes, there is no error, and you get something weird. What can happen is that the computer just throws away any digits beyond 8. So if I take a number like 255, and I add 1 to it, instead of getting 256, I get 0. Because the last bit is just...well...thrown away. So what seems like simple math like 186 plus 92 can yield the impossible answer of 22, not 278.

Back in the 1990s, computers and programmers had a similar issue when for the entire century, years were entered into computers using two digits. So 1985 was entered as 85, 1999 as 99. The 19 part was just assumed. So what happened when 2000 hit? Only the last two digits were stored, so it would be 00, which a computer would translate as 1900.

This problem, called the Y2K bug, or Year 2000 bug, was fixed by having programs changed to store years with the full four digits (or more) instead of just the last two. So we should be just fine until we hit the year 9999.

But how are dates stored in the computer anyway? You guessed it, using binary! In fact, a common way to store dates is to count the number of seconds since a specific date. For many systems and programming languages, dates are stored as the number of seconds after midnight, January 1, 1970. This is stored in a signed 32-bit binary number. It is signed, because computers needed to store dates before 1970, so it used negative numbers to store it. The first digit in a 32-bit number stores the "sign" of the number. Zero for positive, one for negative.

So for years, 32-bit dates have worked out perfectly fine. Each second another bit flips, adding one to the number of seconds that have passed since the start of the decade of disco.

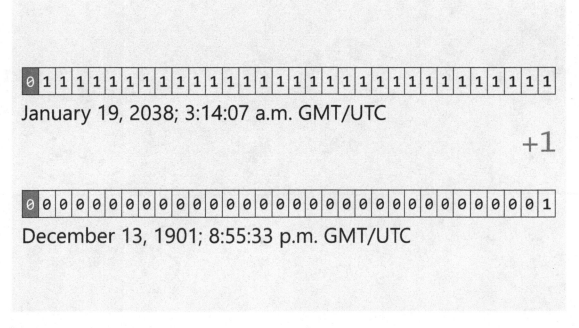

Figure 15-9. Year 2038 bug

Unicode

Using binary, we can represent values of different types in a format that is native to a computer. We can do the same with text; we just have to be a little more creative about how we do it.

Text Encoding

Maybe you have used a decoder ring. Using a decoder ring, you can take a message that contains letters and, using it, find the corresponding number or symbol that is used for that letter. You could take a phrase like this one, and for each unique letter, you have a symbol that represents it. Using this, you can convert each letter to the new code. This is called encoding. You are taking the original text and are converting it to a unique code.

On the other side, if I get a message that uses these symbols, I can take each symbol, and using the same decoder ring, I can match the symbol to the letter and decode the message back into its original format.

Both the encoding and decoding processes need to be identical and agreed upon at both ends. If one end has a different decoder ring than the other, we can't communicate. This agreed-upon method is called a protocol, and it is used at both ends of the communication.

Now, instead of symbols, we can use numbers to represent our protocol. These numbers match uniquely to each character we want to communicate with.

But that is just the simple alphabet. We can represent that as uppercase characters and lowercase characters. Then there is punctuation, common international characters, Greek, special symbols, and block building symbols to draw boxes and lines on the screen.

Plus there are some nonprinted characters like a space, line return, backspace, and others.

© Doug Winnie 2021
D. Winnie, *Essential Java for AP CompSci*, https://doi.org/10.1007/978-1-4842-6183-5_16

You now have a set of unique characters, each with a corresponding number. But remember, computers need to store numbers in binary format, so each of these numbers is converted to a binary, and in this case, we have 256 characters, which are stored in a single byte, or with 8 bits.

ASCII + Unicode

This single byte encoding system is called ASCII or American Standard Code for Information Interchange and was first developed in the early 1960s. Over time, the system expanded to include more characters. But at a certain point, there were too many symbols or glyphs in the world to represent that ASCII wasn't going to cut it anymore.

A new standard called Unicode uses multiple bytes to represent thousands and thousands of symbols from languages all around the world and even ancient symbols and languages from lost civilizations (and even some from science fiction!). The more common characters require fewer bits to store them, which saves space and time when storing or sending them. The lesser or more complex characters require more.

The web is standardized on the UTF-8 format or 8-bit Unicode Transformation Format. It is backward compatible with ASCII. Each character is represented using the prefix U+ and then is followed by a four-digit hexadecimal number. So the letter "D" is U+0044. Four hexadecimal numbers require 2 bytes to store them, or 16 bits. So using just 2 bytes, over 65,000 symbols can be encoded and decoded. This is called Plane 0 of Unicode. For more characters, additional bits are added creating new Planes. Currently, there are three that are mainly used, Plane 0, Plane 1, and Plane 2. There are others that aren't used or can be customized, going up to Plane 16. All in all, the entire breadth of Unicode can store 1,114,112 symbols, called "code points." That's a lot of letters!

Emoji

You use Unicode every day. All of the emoji you use on your phones and devices are symbols in Unicode.

That is why, generally, when emoji are added to one platform, they are added to the other. This is how standards work. In order for a technology to align to a standard, it needs to keep its support for it updated. This includes if it changes and adapts over time.

Variables

Computers have all of the memory, so we have to be able to store something. Right?

To do that in our program, we use variables, but each variable can only handle certain types of values, or literals.

Working with a variable requires we define three things (eventually).

Essentials of Variables

First, we need to determine the type of value we are going to want to store. This is the value type, and we already have encountered a few, like integer, float, string, and more.

Second, we need to give each variable a unique name. Now, variable names have a few rules to them. They must begin with a letter or the $ or _ characters. They are case sensitive. They cannot be a reserved word in Java.

While those are the rules, there are a few recommendations that go along with them. First, you should use camelCase convention, meaning that you concatenate words together, and the first letter is lowercase and each subsequent letter is capitalized. So my name, `Doug Winnie`, would become `dougWinnie`.

Third, we need to assign a value to a variable. That value needs to match the type of the variable, so, for instance, an integer value to an integer variable. We assign that value using the assignment operator, which is the equal sign: =.

Assignment always operates from right to left. Whatever value is on the right is assigned to the variable container we define on the left.

Once we have a variable with a value, we can use it like any literal.

© Doug Winnie 2021
D. Winnie, *Essential Java for AP CompSci*, https://doi.org/10.1007/978-1-4842-6183-5_17

Code Examples

The code on the next page shows examples of working with multiple types of variables in a variety of situations.

This code is also available at the following GitHub repo:

https://github.com/Apress/essential-java-AP-CompSci

Listing 17-1. Working with variables

```java
public class Main {

    public static void main(String[] args) {

        // I: Define a variable
        int quantity;
        double price;
        String name;
        char initial;

        // II: Assign a value to a variable using the assignment operator
        quantity = 5;
        price = 2.50;
        name = "Doug";
        initial = 'W';

        // III: Output a variable
        System.out.printf("%s %s. bought %d items priced at %f each\n",name,
        initial,quantity,price);
        /* Output
        Doug W. bought 5 items priced at 2.500000 each
         */

        // IV: Update value of a variable
        quantity = 10;
        price = 1.99;
        name = "Mike";
        initial = 'J';
```

```java
// V: Output updated variables
System.out.printf("%s %s. bought %d items priced at $%.2f each\n",
name,initial,quantity,price);
/* Output
Mike J. bought 10 items priced at $1.99 each
 */

// VI: Initialize and assign on one line
int myNumber = 5;

// VII: Assign one variable to another
int myValue = myNumber;
    }
}
```

Math!

While there are tons of things that you can do with math in programming and in Java, we are going to cover the essentials here, starting with basic arithmetic operators.

Basic Operators

The basic operators used in Java are for addition, subtraction, multiplication, division, and modulo.

These are all pretty self-explanatory, except for modulo. This essentially is the remainder after division. When you divide two numbers, the remainder is the result of modulo.

Order of Operations

Calculations are based on the algebraic order of operations:

- Groupings are completed first (based on parentheses).
- Multiplicative functions:
    - Multiplication
    - Division
    - Modulo
- Additive functions:
    - Addition
    - Subtraction

Calculations are completed from left to right.

© Doug Winnie 2021
D. Winnie, *Essential Java for AP CompSci*, https://doi.org/10.1007/978-1-4842-6183-5_18

String Concatenation

While you can't "add" strings together, you can combine them to each other. This is called concatenation, and you use the addition symbol.

You can concatenate multiple literal and variable types together. They will all be converted to strings when you do.

Code Examples

The next page shows examples of basic operators for both integer and decimal type values, order of operations, and string concatenation.

This code is also available in the following GitHub repo:

```
https://github.com/Apress/essential-java-AP-CompSci
```

Listing 18-1. Math operators

```java
public class Main {

    public static void main(String[] args) {

        // I: Define and set values for examples
        int a = 2, b = 5, c = 100;
        float foo = 3.0f, bar = 10.5f, baz = 85.25f;

        // Integer Examples
        //
        // II: Addition
        int z = a + b; // 2 + 5 = 7
        System.out.printf("The sum is: %d\n",z);
        // Output: The sum is: 7

        // III: Subtraction
        int y = b - c; // 5 - 100 = -95
        System.out.printf("The difference is: %d\n",y);
        // Output: The difference is: -95

        // IV: Multiplication
        int w = a * c; // 2 * 100 = 200
```

```java
System.out.printf("The product is: %d\n", w);
// Output: The product is: 200

// V: Division
int v = c / b; // 100 / 5 = 20
System.out.printf("The quotient is: %d\n", v);
// Output: The quotient is: 20

// VI: Modulo
int u = b % a; // 5 % 2 = 1
System.out.printf("The remainder is: %d\n", u);
// Output: The remainder is: 1

// VII: Integer division
int t = b / a; // (int)5 / 2 = 2
System.out.printf("The integer quotient is: %d\n", t);
// Output: The integer quotient is: 2

// Float Examples
//
// VIII: Float Multiplication
float qux = foo * bar; // 3.0f * 10.5f = 31.5f
System.out.printf("The float product is: %f\n", qux);
// Output: The float product is: 31.500000

// IX: Float Division
float quux = baz / bar; // 85.25f / 10.5f = 8.119047f
System.out.printf("The float quotient is: %f\n", quux);
// Output: The float quotient is: 8.119047

// X: Integer to Float Division
float quuz = b / a;
System.out.printf("The quotient is: %f\n", quuz);
// Generates a float, but based on the integer quotient
// Output: The quotient is: 2.000000

// XI: Order of operations
int corge = 2 + 5 * 12 + 6 / 2;
System.out.printf("The result is: %d\n", corge);
```

```
// 2 + 60 + 6 / 2
// 2 + 60 + 3
// 62 + 3
// 65
// Output: The result is: 65

int grault = (2 + 5) * (12 + 6) / 2;
System.out.printf("The result is: %d\n", grault);
// 7 * (12 + 6) / 2
// 7 * 18 / 2
// 126 / 2
// 63
// Output: The result is: 63

// XII: String concatenation
String garply = "Doug" + "Winnie";
System.out.println(garply);
// Output: DougWinnie
garply = "Doug" + ' ' + "Winnie";
System.out.println(garply);
// Output: Doug Winnie

// XIII: Concatenation literal
System.out.println("The product of " + a + " and " + b + " is " +
a*b + ".");
// Output: The product of 2 and 5 is 10.
    }
}
```

Math Methods

Basic math operators will only get you so far. There are a bunch more that you can use to do things with more advanced methods like algebra, trigonometry, statistics, calculus, and more in Java.

Working with Simple Methods

The most basic is working with numbers and rounding them. There are three ways to deal with a decimal value on a number.

The first is to just eliminate it entirely. This is called finding the number's floor. Any decimal value is simply removed. Even if it is .99999.

The second is to take any decimal value and raise it up to the next whole number, called the number's ceiling. Any decimal value will move the number to the next whole number. Even if it is .00001.

The last is to do traditional rounding. Anything .5 or higher moves up to the next whole number. Anything below .5 moves down.

To perform these actions, we need to call a method.

A method is a named section of code that we can execute just by calling the name (followed by a pair of parentheses).

Some methods return a value, like our rounding examples mentioned earlier. When a method returns a value, the value that is returned essentially replaces the name of the method when it is called.

In order for most methods to work though, you need to give it something to work with. We provide values to the method by placing them in the pair of parentheses that follows the method name.

© Doug Winnie 2021
D. Winnie, *Essential Java for AP CompSci*, https://doi.org/10.1007/978-1-4842-6183-5_19

Take this example that uses the `ceil()` method to raise any decimal value to the next whole number:

```
double a = 1.25;
double b = Math.ceil(a);
System.out.println(b);
// Output: 2.0
```

The variable a is provided to the `Math.ceil()` method which then performs the ceiling method. It returns a value of `2.0`, which replaces the method call. That value is then assigned to b.

You can put anything that evaluates to a required parameter in a method call, including mathematical operators or other variables. You can even call another method within a method call.

Multiparameter Methods

Some methods like finding the value of a base number raised exponentially need to provide the method with two values. You can provide two values to methods that require it by separating them with a comma:

```
double x = 2.0;
double y = 8.0;
double z = Math.pow(x,y);
System.out.println(z);
// Output: 256
```

Illegal Value Types in Methods

Some methods require specific types of values, or they won't work. IntelliJ will let you know when it encounters a potentially illegal value. If it encounters it when it builds and runs the program, you'll get an error:

```
float foo = 5.5f;
float bar = Math.floor(foo);
// Error, floor() requires a double
```

Math Constants

There are special values that you can refer to by name in Java that represent special irrational numbers that are constant and never change. The most common is π and e.

These are presented by using the phrases `Math.E` and `Math.PI`.

Code Examples

The next page shows examples of basic math methods that you can use in your programs.

This code is also available in the following GitHub repo:

https://github.com/Apress/essential-java-AP-CompSci

Listing 19-1. Common math methods

```java
public class Main {

    public static void main(String[] args) {

        // I: Number methods
        double a = Math.floor(1.99); // a = 1
        double b = Math.ceil(1.01);  // b = 2
        double c = Math.round(1.49); // c = 1
        System.out.printf("Rounding >> floor %f >> ceil %f >> round %f \n",
        a, b, c);
        // Output: Rounding >> floor 1.000000 >> ceil 2.000000 >> round
        1.000000

        // II: Algebraic methods
        double d = Math.pow(2,8);    // d = 256.0
        double e = Math.sqrt(256.0); // e = 128.0
        double f = Math.cbrt(27);    // f = 3.0
        double g = Math.PI;          // Represents pi
        double h = Math.E;           // Represents Euclid's number
        double i = Math.log(50);     // Returns the *natural* logarithm
        double j = Math.log10(50);   // Returns the common (base-10)
                                     logarithm
```

99

```java
        double k = Math.abs(-1);       // k = 1.0
        System.out.printf("%f, %f, %f, %f, %f, %f, %f, %f\n",d,e,f,g,h,
        i,j,k);
        // Output: 256.000000, 16.000000, 3.000000, 3.141593, 2.718282,
        3.912023, 1.698970, 1.000000

        // III: Trigonometric methods
        double l = Math.sin(2);        // Returns sine (using radians)
        double m = Math.cos(2);        // Returns cosine (using radians)
        double n = Math.tan(2);        // Returns tangent (using radians)
        double o = Math.asin(1);       // Returns arc sine (using radians)
        double p = Math.acos(1);       // Returns arc cosine (using radians)
        double q = Math.atan(2);       // Returns arc tangent (using radians)
        double r = Math.toRadians(90.0);          // Returns radians
        double s = Math.toDegrees(Math.PI * 2);     // Returns degrees
        double t = Math.cos(Math.toRadians(Math.PI * 2)); // Nested method
                                                    calls
        System.out.printf("%f, %f, %f, %f, %f, %f, %f, %f,
        %f\n",l,m,n,o,p,q,r,s,t);
        // Output: 0.909297, -0.416147, -2.185040, 1.570796, 0.000000,
        1.107149, 1.570796, 360.000000, 0.993993

        // IV: Comparison methods
        double max = Math.max(1,2);   // Returns 2
        double min = Math.min(1,2);   // Returns 1
        System.out.printf("%f, %f",max,min);
        // Output: 2.000000, 1.000000
    }
}
```

Managing Type

When you work with variables and methods, you need to juggle different value types. Sometimes, you need to work with an integer, but you have a float. Or you have a double that needs to be an integer. How you manage types and force them to be other things is a common part of working with programming languages.

Mixing Types in Evaluations

When you mix types, all values in a mixed evaluation are converted to double before any operations are performed.

Take this, for example:

```
int a = 11;
int b = 4;
double x = 11;
double y = 4;
System.out.print(a / b);
System.out.print(", ");
System.out.print(x / y);
System.out.print(", ");
System.out.print(a / y);
```

The result of this code snippet is

```
2, 2.75, 2.75
```

That is because for the third evaluation, we are combining an integer and a double. When Java sees the mixed types, it converts the integer into a double and completes the operation.

101

© Doug Winnie 2021
D. Winnie, *Essential Java for AP CompSci*, https://doi.org/10.1007/978-1-4842-6183-5_20

Numbers to Strings

Most numeric values when you concatenate within a string will convert to a string without any special treatment. Just "add" them together to another string literal, and the values will concatenate. It is preferable to use the `printf()` method though so you can control and adjust how those values are shown on screen.

```
String a = "Value: " + b;
```

You can't however take a numeric value and simply assign that to a string variable. That's not allowed. Instead, you will need to access a method that is unique for each value type.

For example:

```
Double.toString(value);
Float.toString(value);
Integer.toString(value);
```

When you pass in a value into each of these methods, it will return a string version of that value that you can assign to a string variable.

You'll notice that the value types in these statements are capitalized. There are reasons for this, but we will cover those when we get to classes.

Strings to Numbers

Going the other way is called parsing. You will need to have a method read, or parse, a string and try to see if there is a number value inside of it.

There are limitations though. For instance, the string can only contain decimal points. It cannot contain currency symbols or thousands separators.

Parsing is done with a method that is also attached to a value type name:

```
Double.parseDouble(string);
Float.parseFloat(string);
Integer.parseInt(string);
```

Note the differences between the method names.

Casts

Voila! The rabbit has become a bouquet of flowers!

Casting a spell isn't all that mysterious in Java. In fact, it is a core part of it. Casts are when you treat a value like it is another.

You essentially are trying to force a value to fit a different container. Sometimes, casts won't work however, so be careful when you use them.

Take this example:

```
double foo = 3.00;
int bar = foo;
```

The second line generates an error. Even though the value of foo is, technically, an integer since it has no decimal value, it isn't "strictly" an integer. So the assignment fails.

We can force this by placing a cast before the value we want to treat as a different type. Simply surround a value type in parentheses and put it before the value:

```
int baz = (int) foo;
```

This works with no issues, because the cast is treating foo like an integer so it matches the type.

Cast Errors

There are some pitfalls with casts however. You need to be careful with where you place them, because it can totally change the result of an evaluation:

```
int value1 = 2, value2 = 5;
float q;
q = value2 / value1;
System.out.println(q); // 2.0
```

This example takes two values that are integers and attempts to divide them and assign them to a float variable.

Because they are integers, when they are divided, any decimal is simply thrown away. So the result, 2, is converted into a float (which doesn't require any special handling) and becomes 2.0.

But if we wrap these in a set of parentheses and cast, what should we get?

```
q = (float)(value2 / value1);
System.out.println(q); // 2.0
```

We get the same answer because the integer division is still happening. The two numbers are divided, throwing away the decimal, and then *that* value is cast as a float.

Not very helpful, right?

So, to fix this, we need to cast each value *before* the division happens:

```
q = (float)value2 / (float)value1;
System.out.println(q); // 2.5
```

Code Examples

The next page shows examples of value manipulation and casting that you can use in your programs.

This code is also available in the following GitHub repo:

```
https://github.com/Apress/essential-java-AP-CompSci
```

Listing 20-1. Common value manipulation code

```
public class Main {

    public static void main(String[] args) {

        // NOTE: This code has errors in it and WILL NOT COMPILE

        // Setting variables for examples
        int a = 5;
        double b = 3.14;
        String x = "3.95";
        String y = "185";

        // I: Numbers in string concatenation
        String text = "The value of a is " + a;
        System.out.println(text);
```

```java
// II: Error in direct type conversion
String val = b; // Can't convert types

// III: Convert using the base value type's toString() method
String rate = Double.toString(b);
System.out.println(rate);

// IV: Parse (Convert) a string to a number
double piValue = Double.parseDouble(x);
int qty = Integer.parseInt(y);
double price = Double.parseDouble("$2.50"); // Generates an error

// V: Casting values
double foo = 3.00;
int bar = foo;        // No cast, generates an error
int baz = (int) foo;   // With cast

// VI: Casting issues
int value1 = 2, value2 = 5;
float quotient;

//// without casting:
quotient = value2 / value1;
System.out.println(quotient); // 2.0

//// with improper casting:
quotient = (float)(value2 / value1);
System.out.println(quotient); // 2.0

//// with proper casting:
quotient = (float)value2 / (float)value1;
System.out.println(quotient); // 2.5
    }
}
```

Random Numbers

Rolling a die involves math.

Right? Why would someone ever say that?

Well, in Java and basically in programming, it does. Fortunately, the work is mostly behind the scenes, but we will need to do some work with variables and value types to get it all to work the way we want it.

Create a Random Number Generator

Working with random numbers requires working with a special class called the Random class.

When we work with some classes, like `Math`, we can just work with the class name and a method name after it. This is called a static class. We don't need to do anything special with it. There is a method in the `Math` class we can use, but we are going to learn something new.

When we work with some classes, we can't work with them directly; we need to create an instance of it, which is similar to creating a house from a blueprint in order for us to use it. That is the case for the `Random` class.

Here's how it works:

```
Random rand = new Random();
```

It's a little different than what we have done before. Technically, this is called instantiation. We will get more into what that is later in the class. But here's the gist: we have a class called `Random`, and we are creating a new copy of it and taking that copy and assigning it to a variable container called `rand`.

You'll notice at the top of your code, IntelliJ will add a line called an `import` statement. If this isn't there, it needs to be added at the very first line of the code:

```
import java.util.Random;
```

© Doug Winnie 2021

D. Winnie, *Essential Java for AP CompSci*, https://doi.org/10.1007/978-1-4842-6183-5_21

Now we can refer to all of the methods that are part of the Random class using the name rand (or whatever you call it in your program).

With that, we now have a random number generator that can create any random integer or decimal we want in our program.

<evil cackle laugh>

Random Integers

Creating random integers requires using the nextInt() method of the Random class.

```
Random rand = new Random();
int digit = rand.nextInt(10);
```

In this example, digit will contain a random integer that is *less* than 10. It will never equal 10. That means it can be 0, 1, 2, 3, 4, 5, 6, 7, 8, or 9.

If we want to simulate rolling a die, we will need to adjust the code, ensuring that the number will output the correct possible values.

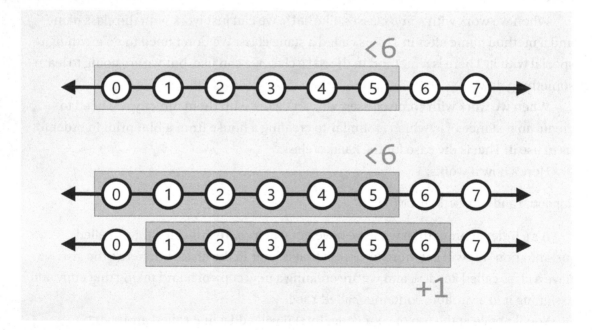

Figure 21-1. *Manipulating number ranges*

If we create a simple random number generator like this one:

```
int die = rand.nextInt(6);
```

We will generate the numbers 0, 1, 2, 3, 4, and 5. However, a die doesn't contain a 0 (at least not any that I have), and the highest number is 6.

So we can fix this by adding 1 to the possible number range:

```
int die = rand.nextInt(6) + 1;
```

Now our possible values for a die are 1, 2, 3, 4, 5, and 6.

Random Decimals

We can also generate random decimals, but the process is a bit different. There is a nextFloat() and nextDouble() method, but we can't define the maximum number.

When you run these methods, you will generate a random decimal between 0 and 1:

```
double decimal = rand.nextDouble();
```

The value of decimal will be between 0 and 1, but never equal 0 or 1.

If we need to adjust this range, we need to manipulate the number range again. We expand it using multiplication (or division) and shift it using addition (or subtraction).

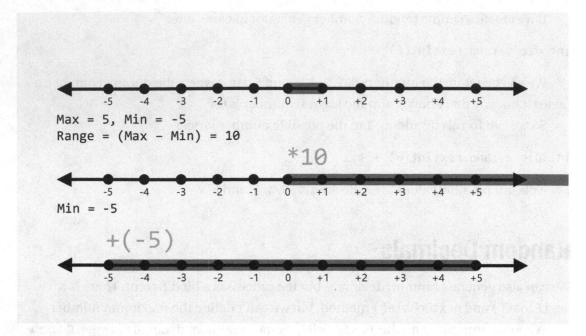

Figure 21-2. *Manipulating decimal ranges*

If we know that the natural range is between 0 and 1, we need to determine the total range of the numbers we need to generate. We can take the difference of the maximum and minimum numbers to determine the range. We then multiply the range by that value.

So now the range is between 0 and 10. We are almost there.

Next, we need to adjust to make it reach the desired minimum. We then add the minimum to the range. So adding a -5 brings the range further to the left. The range is now between -5 and 5.

```
double max = 5;
double min = -5;
double decimal = rand.nextDouble() * (max - min) + min;
```

Code Examples

The next page shows examples of creating random integers and decimal values.

This code is also available in the following GitHub repo:

```
https://github.com/Apress/essential-java-AP-CompSci
```

Listing 21-1. Random number generation

```java
import java.util.Random;

public class Main {

    public static void main(String[] args) {

        // I: Create random number generator
        Random rand = new Random();

        // II: Generate a number from 0 to 9
        int digit = rand.nextInt(10);
        System.out.printf("Random <10: %d \n", digit);

        // III: Roll a die
        int die = rand.nextInt(6) + 1;
        System.out.printf("Random die: %d \n", die);

        // IV: Generate a decimal from -5 to 5
        double max = 5;
        double min = -5;
        double decimal = rand.nextDouble() * (max - min) + min;
        System.out.printf("Random -5 > x < 5: %f \n", decimal);

        // V: Yahtzee Roll
        int die1 = rand.nextInt(6) + 1;
        int die2 = rand.nextInt(6) + 1;
        int die3 = rand.nextInt(6) + 1;
        int die4 = rand.nextInt(6) + 1;
        int die5 = rand.nextInt(6) + 1;
        System.out.printf("Die 1: %d\tDie 2: %d\tDie 3: %d\tDie 4: %d\tDie 5:
        %d", die1, die2, die3, die4, die5);
    }
}
```

SPRINT 22

Capture Input

So far, our programs have been pretty one way. Kinda dull.

To make them more interactive, we need a way to capture input from the user. The most basic way to do that is using the keyboard and have the user input information by typing it in. One of the most fundamental parts of any programming language is the ability to perform standard input and output with a system, sometimes referred to as I/O. So far, we have only performed this one way, using `System.out`; now we can learn the other side of I/O, using `System.in`.

Hello, Scanner

To capture input, we use the `Scanner` class. The `Scanner` can do much more than just work with the keyboard, but we'll get to that later.

Just like with the `Random` class, we need to create a named instance of it, remembering to import it at the top of our code, and we can then use it.

This time, we need to specify what the `Scanner` class is going to use for input. We send output to the screen using `System.out`; so, naturally, we would use `System.in`. This connects us to the input stream of the system, and we can capture that using the `Scanner`:

```
Scanner s = new Scanner(System.in);
```

At the top of our code should be an import statement like this:

```
import java.util.Scanner;
```

Now we can use the variable `s` to trigger the `Scanner` to capture input from the user.

© Doug Winnie 2021
D. Winnie, *Essential Java for AP CompSci*, https://doi.org/10.1007/978-1-4842-6183-5_22

Capturing Strings

To use the Scanner class, we assign a variable with the input captured by the Scanner class instance. When the program encounters this line, it will pause and wait for the user to enter something using the keyboard.

It then takes that input, processes it a little, and then assigns that to the variable:

```
System.out.print("What's your name? ");
String name = s.next();
System.out.printf("Hey there, %s! \n", name);
```

In the preceding example, we display a simple string on the screen. Notice that we use a print() instead of a println(). That will place the cursor at the end of the line so it will look like we are responding to the question directly.

The second line creates a variable called name, typed as a String.

It then accesses the Scanner instance, s, and triggers the next() method. This will capture whatever is entered in with the keyboard until the user presses Enter or Return, and then it sends those characters as a string to the variable name.

We can then send that to the screen.

Capturing Integers

The process is essentially the same for an integer, but since everything is considered a string when we capture it using next(), we need to use a special method called nextInt().

This will parse the input as an integer so it is the correct value type:

```
System.out.print("How many do you wish to buy? ");
int qty = s.nextInt();
System.out.printf("Buying %d items \n", qty);
```

Capturing Decimals

Same thing—a different method, but it will convert to the right format using either nextDouble() or nextFloat():

```java
System.out.print("What is the price? ");
double price = s.nextDouble();
System.out.printf("The item costs $%.2f. \n", price);
```

Code Examples

The next page shows examples of capturing input from the user.

Listing 22-1. Capture input

```java
import java.util.Scanner;

public class Main {

    public static void main(String[] args) {

        // I: Create a scanner, point to the system input
        Scanner s = new Scanner(System.in);

        // II: Capture a string
        System.out.print("What's your name? ");
        String name = s.next();
        System.out.printf("Hey there, %s! \n", name);

        // III: Capture an integer
        System.out.print("How many do you wish to buy? ");
        int qty = s.nextInt();
        System.out.printf("Buying %d items \n", qty);

        // IV: Capture a decimal
        System.out.print("What is the price? ");
        double price = s.nextDouble();
        System.out.printf("The item costs $%.2f. \n", price);
```

```
        // Wrap up
        System.out.printf("%s bought %d items for $%.2f each, totaling
        $%.2f \n", name, qty, price, qty * price);
    }
}
```

SPRINT 23

Creating Trace Tables

Part of programming is thinking like a computer. We already have covered how flowcharts are a big part of programming and planning out what your program will do step by step before you write a line of code.

But you also need to know how your code flows and works as it executes. To do that, we can create a trace table that runs through our code step by step, so we can understand the flow of the code.

It's a Spreadsheet

A trace table is essentially a spreadsheet. You have a minimum of four columns.

The first is a numbered index of all the steps your program runs through.

Seq #	Code	Input	Output/Evaluation	rate	sc	total	commission
Types				double	Scanner	double	double
1	import java.util.Scanner;						
2							
3	public class Main {						
4							
5	public static void main(String[] args) {						
6							
7	// Set commission rate						
8	double rate = .22;			0.22			
9				0.22			
10	// Create scanner			0.22			
11	Scanner sc = new Scanner(System.in);			0.22	Scanner		
12				0.22	Scanner		
13	// Get total			0.22	Scanner		
14	System.out.print("Enter total sales: ");		Enter total sales:	0.22	Scanner		
15	double total = sc.nextDouble();	5750.50		0.22	Scanner	5750.5	
16				0.22	Scanner	5750.5	
17	// Calculate commission			0.22	Scanner	5750.5	
18	double commission = total * rate;		5750.50 * .22 = 1265.11	0.22	Scanner	5750.5	1265.11
19				0.22	Scanner	5750.5	1265.11
20	// Display commission			0.22	Scanner	5750.5	1265.11
21	System.out.printf("Total commission on $%.2f is $%.2f.", total, commission);		Total commission on $5,750.20 is $1,265.11.	0.22	Scanner	5750.5	1265.11
22				0.22	Scanner	5750.5	1265.11
23	}			0.22	Scanner	5750.5	1265.11
24	}			0.22	Scanner	5750.5	1265.11

Figure 23-1. *Example trace table*

The second is the code itself that runs on that line.

The third is the input, if any, that the user puts into the program at that point.

The fourth is the output on the screen or the details of any evaluation that is calculated on that line, for instance, a mathematical formula.

117

© Doug Winnie 2021
D. Winnie, *Essential Java for AP CompSci*, https://doi.org/10.1007/978-1-4842-6183-5_23

The rest of the columns represent all of the variables that you create in the project, with the first row defining the value type of the variable.

Um. Why?

So, why do this? Well, when you take the AP test, you will have *nothing* to help you.

Normally, when you program, you will be able to run and pause your program using a procedure called debugging. Or if there is a problem, the program will end, and you will get some sort of error.

But when you are sitting in the chair, staring at code on the AP test, you won't have any of those to benefit you. So, building your skills to understand program flow completely on your own will be an incredible asset for you as you prep for the exam.

For a while, all of our program assignments will now require creating a trace table. As the projects get more and more complex, we won't do them as much. But for now, most assignments will require you to create a flowchart, the code for the project, and a trace table that will step through all of the code in your project.

Whenever you encounter a situation where you need to input values, you will input them on paper. Random numbers you will generate on your own. But in the end, you will step through every line of code from beginning to end.

Methods

Methods are named sections of code that you can use to repeat actions multiple times by referring to the method name.

Methods have similar rules to variable names where you can't start them with numbers or special characters. Methods are named using camelCase just like variables.

Method Basics

When you call a method, you provide the method name followed by a pair of parentheses. Later, we will learn how to use these parentheses to provide values to work with inside the method.

You can think of calling a method as replacing that method name with the lines of code within it from where it was called. This will come in handy when we talk about methods that can return values later on.

Listing 24-1. Calling a method

```
public static void main(String[] args) {
    displayMsg();
}
```

Writing a Method

We define a method outside of the `main()` method in our program code. It is important to place it outside of the `main()` method, but still keep it within the `Main` program class.

A method needs to define what type of method it is; you define that at the beginning of the method declaration.

119

© Doug Winnic 2021
D. Winnie, *Essential Java for AP CompSci*, https://doi.org/10.1007/978-1-4842-6183-5_24

Listing 24-2. Writing a method

```
public static void displayMsg() {
    System.out.println("This is within the method");
}
```

In the preceding method definition, you start with a reserved word like `private` and `static`. This determines the amount of access that a user has to a method call. Right now, all of our code is in the same file, or class, but later when we define our own custom classes, we will change how this works. Notice that it matches the reserved words before the `main()` class listed earlier.

The next word, `void`, defines what type of value the method returns when it is finished. Our method doesn't return a value, so we state that using the `void` statement. Later, we will change this with the value type that is returned by the method.

Finally, we create a matching pair of braces and place the code that will run when the method calls inside it.

Call a Method

In the `main()` method, we can call the method in our project by entering just the method name followed by a pair of parentheses. Make sure there is no space between the method name and the parentheses.

Method Flow

When you build and run the program, the contents of the `main()` method will run as usual. When it encounters the method call, it diverts the flow of the execution of code to within the code in the method.

In the method, it then executes the code inside of it, in this case display a statement on the screen.

Code Guide

The following code guide shows you an example method and how to create and call it.

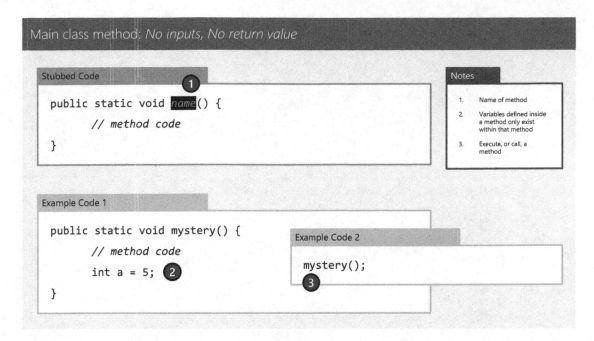

Figure 24-1. *Main class method: no inputs, no return value*

Code Examples

The next page shows examples of capturing input from the user.

This code is also available in the following GitHub repo:

`https://github.com/Apress/essential-java-AP-CompSci`

Listing 24-3. Simple method

```java
public class Main {

    public static void main(String[] args) {
        displayMsg();
    }

    public static void displayMsg() {
        System.out.println("This is within the method");
    }

}
```

Calling Methods Within Methods

Methods can be called within each other as well. When you enter a method within another method, you are digging deeper into the code, and when that inner method ends, you return to the method that called it.

Be careful not to have infinite recursion, where you call a method within itself!

Methods Within Methods

When you call methods within methods, you are going deeper into the operation of the program. At each level, when you go deeper, you need to step out of it in the order you step in.

Like this code:

Listing 25-1. Nested methods

```
public static void main(String[] args) {
    outMethod();
    System.out.println();
    inMethod();
}

public static void outMethod() {
    System.out.println("Outer Method");
    inMethod();
}
```

123

© Doug Winnie 2021

D. Winnie, *Essential Java for AP CompSci*, https://doi.org/10.1007/978-1-4842-6183-5_25

```
public static void inMethod() {
    System.out.println("Inner Method");
}
```

The code starts in the main() method. When it encounters the outMethod() call, it steps into the outMethod() and displays the message "Outer Method".

Inside of that method, it encounters the call for inMethod(). It then steps deeper into the program and executes the content of the inMethod().

When that method ends, it returns to where the program previously was, which was in the outMethod(). Then that method ends, and it returns to the main() method.

There, it prints a blank line on the screen and executes the inMethod() again. This time, when it executes it, it brings the program flow back to the main() method when it is finished.

Then the program ends.

Infinite Methods

When you place a reference to a method within itself, you can cause an infinite recursion. Recursion means that you are finding a solution to a problem by solving smaller instances of the same problem. We will learn more about recursion later in this course, but recursion always requires a way for the solution to end.

Listing 25-2. Infinite recursion

```
public static void infiniteMethod() {
    System.out.println("This goes on forever!");
    infiniteMethod();
}
```

In the preceding example, the method infiniteMethod() is called within itself, with no way to end the cycle, creating an infinite loop.

Code Examples

The next page shows examples of capturing input from the user.

This code is also available in the following GitHub repo:

```
https://github.com/Apress/essential-java-AP-CompSci
```

Listing 25-3. Nested and infinite method examples

```java
public class Main {

    public static void main(String[] args) {
        outMethod();
        System.out.println();
        inMethod();
    }

    public static void outMethod() {
        System.out.println("Outer Method");
        inMethod();
    }

    public static void inMethod() {
        System.out.println("Inner Method");
    }

    public static void infiniteMethod() {
        System.out.println("This goes on forever!");
        infiniteMethod();
    }

}
```

Methods and Values

Methods serve as engines that can process things for you and give you results that you can work with. Like any engine, you need to provide it something to work with.

Methods provide input and output capabilities. Input values are defined in the method definition, and output values are sent out using the return statement.

Accepting Values in Methods

A method can accept values to use within the method. To define a method to accept values, you need to state what type the values coming into it are and what variable name is used for the values in the method.

Listing 26-1. Accepting values in methods

```
public static void average(float val1, float val2, float val3)
{
    float avg = val1 + val2 + val3;
    avg = avg / 3;
    System.out.println(avg);
}
```

In this example, the average() method is expecting three values, each of which is defined as a float.

To call this method, you would pass in the values in the method call:

```
average(10,15,12);
```

The flow of the program then goes into the average() method and pulls in the values that are passed in. The variables defined in the method definition are then used to temporarily store the values of the passed in values until the method is finished. The variables are then discarded at that point.

© Doug Winnie 2021
D. Winnie, *Essential Java for AP CompSci*, https://doi.org/10.1007/978-1-4842-6183-5_26

Returning a Value

A method can also return a value from where it was originally called. This will take the functional call statement and replace it with the value that is returned from the method when it is completed.

To create a method with a returned value, you need to define the return value type and then use the return statement and send the value you want to return from the method.

Listing 26-2. Returning a value

```
public static float avgValue(float val1, float val2, float val3)
{
    float avg = val1 + val2 + val3;
    avg = avg / 3;
    return avg;
}
```

In this case, the method doesn't display anything, but it returns a value after processing it.

The returned value essentially replaces the method call itself in the original code, and you can place it wherever you can supply a variable or literal. It just needs to match the expected type which is defined by the return type in the method definition.

Overloading a Method

If you have multiple numbers of values you need to accept, but need to use the same method name, you can overload it by providing multiple definitions for the same method name with different incoming value types or number of incoming value types.

Listing 26-3. Overloading a method

```
public static float avgValue(float val1, float val2, float val3)
{
    float avg = val1 + val2 + val3;
```

```
    avg = avg / 3;
    return avg;
}

public static float avgValue(float val1, float val2)
{
    float avg = val1 + val2;
    avg = avg / 2;
    return avg;
}
```

In this case, if I executed

```
System.out.println(avgValue(10,15,12));
```

the first method would run, since it accepts three values.
If I executed

```
System.out.println(avgValue(10,15));
```

the second method would run.

You can overload methods with different quantities of method parameters or with different value types of parameters to accommodate multiple types of values.

Your value types don't need to be the same, and the incoming and outgoing value types can be different.

Listing 26-4. Different parameter and return types

```
public static float intDiv(int val1, int val2)
{
    float quot = (float)val1 / (float)val2;
    return quot;
}
```

Code Guides

Here are multiple examples on how to work with methods that accept, return, and can handle different sets of input variables using overloading.

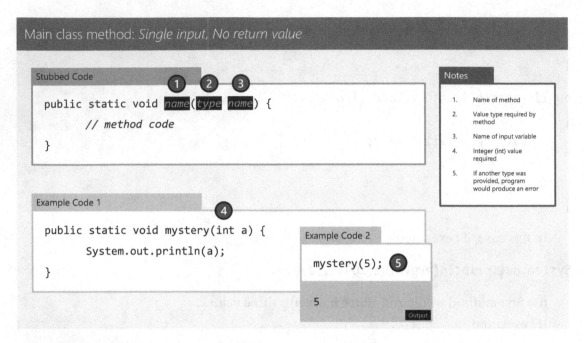

Figure 26-1. *Main class method: single input, no return value*

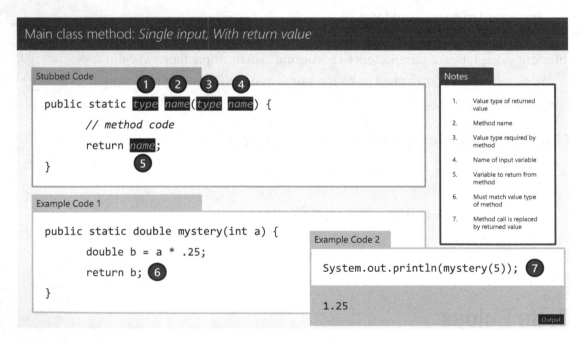

Figure 26-2. *Main class method: single input, with return value*

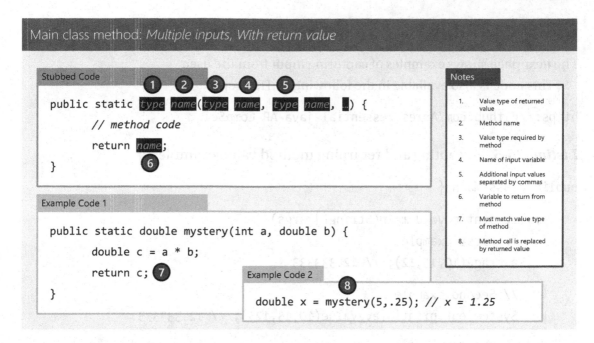

Figure 26-3. *Main class method: multiple inputs, with return value*

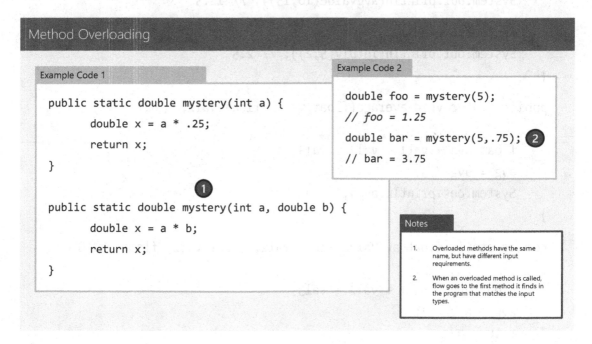

Figure 26-4. *Method overloading*

Code Examples

The next page shows examples of capturing input from the user.

This code is also available in the following GitHub repo:

https://github.com/Apress/essential-java-AP-CompSci

Listing 26-5. Accepting and returning method value examples

```java
public class Main {

    public static void main(String[] args) {
        // First example
        average(10,15,12); // 12.333333

        // Second example
        System.out.println(avgValue(10,15,12)); // 12.333333

        // Third example
        System.out.println(avgValue(10,15)); // 12.5

        // Fourth example
        System.out.println(intDiv(5,2)); // 2.5
    }

    public static void average(float val1, float val2, float val3)
    {
        float avg = val1 + val2 + val3;
        avg = avg / 3;
        System.out.println(avg);
    }

    public static float avgValue(float val1, float val2, float val3)
    {
        float avg = val1 + val2 + val3;
        avg = avg / 3;
        return avg;
    }
```

```
public static float avgValue(float val1, float val2)
{
    float avg = val1 + val2;
    avg = avg / 2;
    return avg;
}

public static float intDiv(int val1, int val2)
{
    float quot = (float)val1 / (float)val2;
    return quot;
}

}
```

Methods and Scope

Variable scope defines where in your program a variable exists for statements and other variables to have access to it to work.

Variable Scope Errors

Where variables are defined can affect what can access the values stored inside of them. This is defined by the variable's scope. In the following code, myMainValue is not accessible from myMethod() because its scope is restricted to main().

Listing 27-1. Variable out of scope

```
public static void main(String[] args) {
    // This variable exists only in the main() method of the program
    int myMainValue = 10;
}

public static void myMethod() {
    System.out.println(myMainValue);
}
```

Defining Class-Scoped Variables

You can define a variable to be scoped to a class, meaning that any method that is within that class can access it without any issues.

To define a class-scoped variable, define it before the main method declaration. Often, you might want to define the variable at first and not give it a value until the main method executes.

135

© Doug Winnie 2021
D. Winnie, *Essential Java for AP CompSci*, https://doi.org/10.1007/978-1-4842-6183-5_27

Listing 27-2. Defining a class-scoped variable

```
public static int myMainValue;

public static void main(String[] args) {
    myMainValue = 10;
}

public static void myMethod() {
    System.out.println(myMainValue);
}
```

Class Conflicts

You can sometimes create conflicts between scopes based on the design of your methods.

When you pass in a value to a method, you are creating a copy of the value and are not linking to the original variable.

Listing 27-3. Variable scope issue with class

```
public static double myValue;
public static double myOtherValue;

public static void main(String[] args) {
    // This variable exists only in the main() method of the program
    myValue = 10.0;
    myOtherValue = 12.5;

    System.out.printf("myValue = %.2f and myOtherValue = %.2f.\n",
    myValue,myOtherValue);

    System.out.println("------------------ Starting method");
    myMethod(myValue,myOtherValue);
    System.out.println("----------------- Returning from method");

    System.out.printf("myValue = %.2f and myOtherValue = %.2f.\n",
    myValue,myOtherValue);
```

```
    // System.out.printf("value1 = %.2f and value2 = %.2f.\n",
    value1,value2);
}

public static void myMethod(double value1, double value2) {
    // Take the values coming into the method and change them
    System.out.printf("value1 = %.2f and value2 = %.2f.\n", value1,value2);

    value1 += 10.2;
    value2 += 5.5;

    System.out.printf("value1 = %.2f and value2 = %.2f.\n", value1,value2);
    System.out.printf("myValue = %.2f and myOtherValue = %.2f.\n",
    myValue,myOtherValue);

    // create a product
    double product = value1 * value2;
    System.out.println(String.format("The product is %.2f", product));
}
```

When you run this program, the values you pass in are copied, and when they are changed within the method, they have no effect on the original values that are defined in the class.

Here is the output:

```
myValue = 10.00 and myOtherValue = 12.50.
------------------ Starting method
value1 = 10.00 and value2 = 12.50.
value1 = 20.20 and value2 = 18.00.
myValue = 10.00 and myOtherValue = 12.50.
The product is 363.60
------------------ Returning from method
myValue = 10.00 and myOtherValue = 12.50.
```

When the original two values are passed in, there is no link between the variables inside the method and the variables defined in the class. So the values of 20.2 and 18.0 only exist in the method.

137

Code Examples

The next page shows examples of capturing input from the user.

This code is also available in the following GitHub repo:

https://github.com/Apress/essential-java-AP-CompSci

Listing 27-4. Scope and copied values

```
public class Main {

    public static double myValue;
    public static double myOtherValue;

    public static void main(String[] args) {
        // This variable exists only in the main() method of the program
        myValue = 10.0;
        myOtherValue = 12.5;

        System.out.printf("myValue = %.2f and myOtherValue = %.2f.\n",
        myValue,myOtherValue);

        System.out.println("------------------ Starting method");
        myMethod(myValue,myOtherValue);
        System.out.println("----------------- Returning from method");

        System.out.printf("myValue = %.2f and myOtherValue = %.2f.\n",
        myValue,myOtherValue);
        // System.out.printf("value1 = %.2f and value2 = %.2f.\n",
        value1,value2);
    }

    public static void myMethod(double value1, double value2) {
        // Take the values coming into the method and change them
        System.out.printf("value1 = %.2f and value2 = %.2f.\n",
        value1,value2);

        value1 += 10.2;
        value2 += 5.5;
```

```java
System.out.printf("value1 = %.2f and value2 = %.2f.\n",
value1,value2);
System.out.printf("myValue = %.2f and myOtherValue = %.2f.\n",
myValue,myOtherValue);

// create a product
double product = value1 * value2;
System.out.println(String.format("The product is %.2f", product));
    }
}
```

Boolean Values and Equality

You have heard that everything with computers comes down to binary, or yes and no answers. That is true, and you can use that in your programs using Boolean values and logic operators. Boolean variables contain, and only contain, the values `true` or `false`. To determine a true or false response, there are a number of operators called logic operators that evaluate an equation as either `true` or `false`. You can then take that value and work with it or assign it to a Boolean variable.

Creating a Boolean Variable

Boolean variables can only contain two values: `true` or `false`. To create one, you initialize the variable using the `Boolean` value type like this:

```
Boolean a;
```

You can then assign a value of `true` or `false` to the variable:

```
a = true;
```

Setting a Boolean variable using a literal is just one way that you can assign a value, but it isn't the most flexible way. Instead, the use of logic operators tests a number of scenarios to determine if a test, or condition, is true or false, and then the result of that test is assigned to the Boolean variable as `true` or `false` values.

141

© Doug Winnie 2021
D. Winnie, *Essential Java for AP CompSci*, https://doi.org/10.1007/978-1-4842-6183-5_28

Boolean Logic Operators

The main Boolean logic operators function on principles of mathematics. Basic operators compare two, and only two, values against each other. Values are then determined to be either equal, not equal, greater than, less than, or a combination of these to another value.

```
int a = 5;
Boolean result;
result = (a == 5); // Equality, result true
result = (a != 5); // Inequality, result false
result = (a > 5);  // Greater than, result is false
result = (a < 5);  // Less than, result is false
result = (a <= 5); // Greater than or equal to, result is true
result = (a >= 5); // Less than or equal to, result is true
```

Altering a Boolean Value

You can reverse the value of any Boolean evaluation or variable by using the Not operator, represented by an exclamation point added as a prefix to a value, variable or evaluation. Simply place it immediately before the evaluation or variable:

```
int a = 5;
Boolean result;
result = (a == 5);  // result true
result = !result;   // result false
result = !(a == 5); // result false
```

Combining Logic with Evaluations

In addition to literals and variables, you can use evaluations to determine Boolean values. Logic operators are always performed last in the order of operations (before the assignment operator), so you can create groupings of evaluations using parentheses to create more complex scenarios, including the use of values returned from methods.

```
int a = 5;
Boolean result;
result = (5 + 5) > 10; // false
```

Compound Logic Operators

To create more complex evaluations, you can use the logical "AND" and "OR" operators. For OR, any one of the values needs to be true for the entire evaluation to be true. For AND, all values need to be true for the entire evaluation to be true.

```
int a = 5;
Boolean result;
result = (a < 5) || (a / 2 < 5); // OR: true
result = (a < 5) && (a / 2 < 5); // AND: false
```

Code Examples

The next page shows examples of capturing input from the user.

This code is also available in the following GitHub repo:

```
https://github.com/Apress/essential-java-AP-CompSci
```

Listing 28-1. Example Boolean logic code

```
public class Main {

    public static void main(String[] args) {
        int a = 5;
        Boolean result;

        System.out.println("Basic operators");

        result = (a == 5); // Equality, result true
        display(result);

        result = (a != 5); // Inequality, result false
        display(result);
```

```
result = (a > 5);  // Greater than, result is false
display(result);

result = (a < 5);  // Less than, result is false
display(result);

result = (a >= 5); // Greater than or equal to, result is true
display(result);

result = (a <= 5); // Less than or equal to, result is true
display(result);

System.out.println("Not operator");

result = !result;  // Not operator, true becomes false
display(result);

result = !true;    // true becomes false
display(result);

result = !(a < 5); // false becomes true
display(result);

System.out.println("Evaluations and returned values");

result = (5 + 5) > 10; // false
display(result);

result = getNumber() < .5; // true or false, depends on the value
                                returned
display(result);

System.out.println("OR");

result = true || true;   // true
display(result);

result = true || false;  // true
display(result);

result = false || true;  // true
display(result);
```

```java
        result = false || false; // false
        display(result);

        result = (a < 5) || (a / 2 < 5); // true
        display(result);

        System.out.println("AND");

        result = true && true;    // true
        display(result);

        result = true && false;   // false
        display(result);

        result = false && true;   // false
        display(result);

        result = false && false; // false
        display(result);

        result = (a < 5) && (a / 2 < 5); // false
        display(result);
    }
    public static void display(boolean result) {
        System.out.println("The result is " + result);
    }
    public static void display(double result) {
        System.out.println("The value is " + result);
    }
    public static double getNumber() {
        double rand = Math.random();
        display(rand);
        return rand;
    }
}
```

Simple Conditional Statements

Boolean values give us the building blocks to do different things based on their true or false answers. The roads we need to drive down based on those values are called conditional statements. These statements route the flow of the code based on the values of Boolean variables, evaluations, or returned values from methods.

The basic set of conditional statements consist of the `if`, `else if`, and `else` statements.

The if Statement

The `if` statement is paired with a parenthesis-wrapped value that will be either `true` or `false`. If the condition is `true`, the code inside the code block after it will execute. If it is `false`, the code block will be skipped, and the program flow will continue.

```
if (conditional) {
    // code goes here
}
```

The else Statement

If you want to perform an alternate action if the original condition evaluates to `false`, you can add an `else` statement with another matching code block after the code block for the `if` statement:

© Doug Winnie 2021
D. Winnie, *Essential Java for AP CompSci*, https://doi.org/10.1007/978-1-4842-6183-5_29

```
if (conditional) {
    // this code runs if the conditional is true
} else {
    // this code runs if the conditional is false
}
```

The else if Statement

You can also string together conditional statements using the else if statement, providing multiple conditional tests. These tests are run in a chain. If a condition in the chain is found to be true, the matching code block runs, and then the rest of the chain is completely ignored. You can have as many else if statements as you want in the chain, but there can only be one if statement, and the else is optional (depending on the logic you are trying to process):

```
if (conditional) {
    // this code runs if the conditional is true
} else if (conditional) {
    // this code runs if the second conditional is true
} else {
    // this code runs if both conditionals are false
}
```

Understanding Conditional Flow

Depending on how you build the chain, or chains, the flow of your program will change. If you create a chain of if statements, they will all be tested, regardless if any of them are false. If you have a single if statement and the rest are else if statements, if one is true, then anything after that is skipped in the chain.

You can nest conditional statements inside of each other using the code block braces:

```
if (x == 1) {
    if (y == 1) {
        // Both x and y are 1
```

```
    } else if (y == 2) {
        // x is 1 and y is 2
    } else {
        // x is 1 and y is not 1 or 2
} else if (x == 2) {
    if (y == 1) {
        // x is 2, and y is 1
    } else if (y == 2) {
        // x is 2, and y is 2
    } else {
        // x is 2 and y is not 1 or 2
} else {
    // x is not 1 or 2, y could be anything
}
```

Code Examples

The next page shows examples of capturing input from the user.

This code is also available in the following GitHub repo:

https://github.com/Apress/essential-java-AP-CompSci

Listing 29-1. Example if, else, and else if statement code

```java
public class Main {

    public static void main(String[] args) {
        // Basic if example
        if (true) {
            // code here will always run
        }

        if (false) {
            // code here will never run
        }
```

```
    // Basic if...else example
    if (true) {
        // code here will always run
    } else {
        // code here will never run
    }

    if (false) {
        // code here will never run
    } else {
        // code here will always run
    }

    // Basic if, else if, else example
    int a = 5;

    if (a == 5) {
        // code here will run if the condition is true
        // then the entire if/else if/else block ends
    } else if (a == 4) {
        // code here will run if the second condition is true
        // then the rest of the if/elsef/else block ends
    } else {
        // code here will run if none of the previous conditions are
        true
    }

    // Complete examples

    int x = 5;
    if (x > 3) {
        disp("X is larger than 3");
    } else if (x > 1) {
        disp("X is larger than 1");
    } else {
        disp("X is not larger than 3 or 1");
    }

}
```

```java
    public static void disp(String msg) {
        System.out.println(msg);
    }
}
/* Output: X is larger than 3 */
```

Matching Conditions with the switch Statement

The switch statement is an alternative conditional structure that looks for matching cases in a series and executes a set of code for the matching case statement. A user can also define a default case if none of the cases match the condition defined in the case statement.

Instead of using logical operators to determine true or false answers, the switch statement compares a specific value (or returned value) against the list of cases. If a match is found, it runs the associated code. That section of code needs to end with the break statement to complete the section of code.

Creating a switch Statement Code Block

The switch statement includes the variable, expression, or returned value in a set of parentheses. It is then followed by a single code block:

```
switch (variable) {
    //
}
```

Inside the code block, you create a case using the case statement followed by the matching value and end with a colon and then the lines of code. Then you end the section with a break statement:

```
switch (variable) {
    case 1:
        // code if variable is equal to 1
        break;
}
```

153

© Doug Winnie 2021
D. Winnie, *Essential Java for AP CompSci*, https://doi.org/10.1007/978-1-4842-6183-5_30

You can add multiple case statements for a single section of code:

```
switch (variable) {
    case 'A':
    case 'a':
        // code if variable is equal to A or a
        break;
}
```

Additional cases are added after the break statement for each one:

```
switch (variable) {
    case 'A':
    case 'a':
        // code if variable is equal to A or a
        break;
    case 'B':
    case 'b':
        // code if variable is equal to B or b
        break;
}
```

If none of the cases match, you can use a default statement to catch anything that doesn't match the earlier cases:

```
switch (variable) {
    case 'A:
    case 'a':
        // code if variable is equal to A or a
        break;
    case 'B':
    case 'b':
        // code if variable is equal to B or b
        break;
    default:
        // code if none of the cases match
        break;
}
```

Things to Look Out for with the switch Statement

Common issues with the switch statement include

- Forgetting the break statement at the end of the code associated with a case statement.

- Putting logical operators in the switch statement that evaluates as a Boolean vs. simply containing the variable you want to test against.

- The switch statement is a good option if you are asking for input from the user to make a selection, like from a menu of options.

Code Examples

The next page shows examples of capturing input from the user.

This code is also available in the following GitHub repo:

https://github.com/Apress/essential-java-AP-CompSci

Listing 30-1. Example switch statement code

```java
import java.util.Scanner;

public class Main {

    public static Scanner sc;

    public static void main(String[] args) {
            sc = new Scanner(System.in);

            displayMenu();

        // The charAt() method extracts the first character of a string.
        // This is an example of chaining statements together.
            char selection = sc.next().charAt(0);

            processSelection(selection);
    }
```

```java
public static void displayMenu() {
    System.out.println("Main Menu");
    System.out.println("==================");
    System.out.println("A: Display Greeting");
    System.out.println("B: Display Compliment");
    System.out.println("C: Display Farewell");
    System.out.println("==================");
    System.out.print("Command? ");
}

public static void processSelection(char selection) {
    String output;
    switch (selection) {
        case 'A':
        case 'a':
            output = "Hello there!";
            break;
        case 'B':
        case 'b':
            output = "You look great today!";
            break;
        case 'C':
        case 'c':
            output = "See you soon!";
            break;
        default:
            output = "Invalid command";
            break;
    }

    System.out.println(output);
}
}
```

The Ternary Operator

One of the most common actions when creating conditional statements is to generate a unique value if a condition evaluates as a Boolean true or false. To make this more concise, a unique operator called the ternary operator allows you to perform a conditional action and generate a unique value that you can use in your program in a single line of code.

The if-else Statement Equivalent

Take the following code as an example of a simple if...else statement that assigns a value:

```
int result;
boolean test = false;

if (test) {
    result = 1;
} else {
    result = 0;
}
```

In this example, the variable test will contain a Boolean value, and the if statement will test the value. Since the value will be false, the integer variable result is the number 0.

© Doug Winnie 2021
D. Winnie, *Essential Java for AP CompSci*, https://doi.org/10.1007/978-1-4842-6183-5_31

Converting to a Ternary Operator

This can be simplified using the ternary operator, sometimes simplified using the two characters unique to the operator ?:.

The operator starts by evaluating a condition, and if the ? and : characters are present, it triggers the operator. After the conditional, the ? character defines the value that is returned if the condition is true. After the :, the value is returned if the condition is false:

```
result = conditional ? true option : false option;
```

Using this, the preceding if...else statement could be rewritten in a single line of code:

```
result = test ? 1 : 0;
```

Because the value of test is false, the value after the colon, 0, is then used and is assigned to the variable result. If the value of test is true, the 1 after the question mark is used and assigned to result.

Using the Ternary Operator Inline with Code

While it is most common to assign a value using the ternary operator, you can also use it inline to provide a Boolean option based on a conditional:

```
System.out.println((value < 5) ? "Value is less than 5" : "Value is not less than 5");
```

In this example, if value is less than five, the first phrase after the question mark is displayed. If value is not less than five, the second phrase after the color is displayed.

Code Examples

The next page shows examples of capturing input from the user.

This code is also available in the following GitHub repo:

```
https://github.com/Apress/essential-java-AP-CompSci
```

Listing 31-1. Example ternary operator code

```java
public class Main {

    public static void main(String[] args) {
        // Basic example
        int result;
        boolean test = false;

        if (test) {
            result = 1;
        } else {
            result = 0;
        }

        System.out.println("The result is " + result);

        result = test ? 1 : 0;

        System.out.println("The result is " + result);

        // Logic operator example

        int value = 5;
        String msg;

        if (value < 5) {
            msg = "Value is less than 5";
        } else {
            msg = "Value is not less than 5";
        }

        System.out.println(msg);

        msg = (value < 5) ? "Value is less than 5" : "Value is not less
        than 5";
        System.out.println(msg);
```

```
      // Inline example

      System.out.println((value < 5) ? "Value is less than 5" : "Value is
      not less than 5");
  }
}
/* Output

The result is 0
The result is 0
Value is not less than 5
Value is not less than 5
Value is not less than 5

*/
```

The Stack and the Heap

When we work with memory and values in computers, we have to distinguish between two ways the computer stores values and how variables keep track of them. One way is using the stack, which is an orderly way to organize data that is a consistent size. The second way is using the heap, which can handle data and values of variable size and provide pointers to where to get the values.

Understanding the Stack

Picture a distribution center. There is a giant room filled with rows and rows of products that are organized for workers and automated drones to acquire items and prepare them to ship to customers.

Each item occupies a specific amount of space on the shelf. This predictable size allows the center managers to know how much can be stored on each shelf and row.

Computer memory can work in the same way. When we create a variable, we are reserving space in memory for the value. The type of value we create defines how much space in memory we need to reserve for the value.

This is why we need to provide the type of value when we define a variable. The computer needs to know how much memory to save for the value we are about to store.

Take, for instance, an integer value. An integer is a 32-bit value. It occupies 32 bits or 4 bytes of memory to store the value. That amount of space never changes. It will never be more or less than 32 bits in size.

When we organize multiple values in memory, we create an organized arrangement of all of the reserved space allocated for each value. The variable value is equal to the value stored in that location in memory.

When a value is no longer needed, there is a process called "garbage collection" that goes through memory and removes values that aren't needed anymore, making it available for future variables that are created.

© Doug Winnie 2021
D. Winnie, *Essential Java for AP CompSci*, https://doi.org/10.1007/978-1-4842-6183-5_32

Understanding the Heap

The heap, however, is a completely different way to store values in the computer.

Instead of an orderly stack, with direct access to values and variables, the heap needs to work with values that will vary in size and length. Take a string, for example. A string can contain a single letter, or it can contain a complete novel if you wanted it to. Because of this variability of length, a different type of system needs to be created to store this type of value.

The heap is exactly like it sounds. Values of varying lengths and sizes are thrown onto a pile. Each item on the pile has an identifier. This is a memory address that the program stores in the variable for the value. For a value stored on the heap, there are actually two values.

The first is the value of where in memory the data is stored. The second is the actual data, stored at the location in memory that is indicated.

Why This All Matters

So why is this all important? Because what is stored in a variable for a value on the stack is the value itself, like the value of an integer.

The value for a variable on the heap is only the reference to where the value is stored. When you access a variable, like a String, it is performing two actions, finding the memory address for a value and then accessing what is stored at that address.

So what happens when you compare values from the heap? There is a distinct possibility that even though two heap-stored values contain the same values, the fact that they are at different memory addresses means that the variable values themselves aren't equal to each other.

Testing Equality with Strings

When comparing strings together, there are some issues that can come up. When you work with primitive local value types like int, float, etc., these are stored as values on the stack that have unique memory addresses from each other. When you work with class types, like String, they refer to memory locations on the heap. When you use the equality operator, ==, it looks and returns true if the reference is equal between the two items. Sometimes, when you use class types, the references can be different, so this returns a false, even if the values in the strings are identical.

Alternatively, you can use the equals() method to compare two items entirely based on value and ignore if their references are different.

When the Heap Throws Equality

Take this example, which returns true using the simple equality operator:

```
String a = "CompSci";
String b = "CompSci";

// Result is true, because the references are identical
boolean result = (a == b);
System.out.println("The result of a == b is " + result);
```

The strings a and b have the same reference because the memory for the String literal "CompSci" is created first and both strings refer to the same memory address that holds the literal value.

163

© Doug Winnie 2021
D. Winnie, *Essential Java for AP CompSci*, https://doi.org/10.1007/978-1-4842-6183-5_33

If we create unique instances of the String class using the new statement, we can see where the problems come up. The following example returns false:

```
String c = new String("CompSci");
String d = new String("CompSci");

// Result is false, because the references are different
result = (c == d);
System.out.println("The result of c == d is " + result);
```

The result is false, because we create the strings first using the new statement, which creates two completely different references. Since the equality operator in this case is looking for identical references, the result is false since they are both different.

How to Better Compare String Values

Confusing, I know. But there is an easy way to clean this up. We can use the equals() method on the String variable we want to compare and provide the variable or literal we want to compare the value to:

```
String c = new String("CompSci");
String d = new String("CompSci");

// Result is true, because the values are identical
result = c.equals(d);
System.out.println("The result of c.equals(d) is " + result);
```

You can also use a literal in this example:

```
// Result is true, because the values are identical
result = c.equals("CompSci");
System.out.println("The result of c.equals(\"CompSci\") is " + result);
```

When comparing two strings together, it is usually safe if you are comparing a string variable and a string literal using the equality operator, ==. However, if you are comparing two string variables together, it can often be better to use the equals() method to compare them to avoid reference confusion and odd results in your code.

Code Examples

The next page shows examples of capturing input from the user.

This code is also available in the following GitHub repo:

```
https://github.com/Apress/essential-java-AP-CompSci
```

Listing 33-1. Comparing strings

```java
public class Main {

    public static void main(String[] args) {
        // Issue with == and strings
        // New strings that are built using literals
        String a = "CompSci";
        String b = "CompSci";

        // Result is true, because the references are identical
        boolean result = (a == b);
        System.out.println("The result of a == b is " + result);

        // New strings that are built as instances of a class
        String c = new String("CompSci");
        String d = new String("CompSci");

        // Result is false, because the the references are different
        result = (c == d);
        System.out.println("The result of c == d is " + result);

        // Result is true, because the values are identical
        result = c.equals(d);
        System.out.println("The result of c.equals(d) is " + result);

        // Result is true, because the values are identical
        result = c.equals("CompSci");
        System.out.println("The result of c.equals(\"CompSci\") is " +
        result);
    }
}
```

```
/* Output

The result of a == b is true
The result of c == d is false
The result of c.equals(d) is true
The result of c.equals("CompSci") is true

*/
```

Dealing with Errors

When you introduce input from users, they won't always provide input that is going to work for your program. When that happens, you need a way to have the program recognize that something is wrong and address it, without completely crashing.

When a program encounters an error, it "throws" it. You can then "catch" the error and do something with it, usually to provide some feedback for the user to know what they did wrong.

Coding to Catch Errors

To start, you need to wrap the code you think could cause an error. Begin with the `try` statement and create a code block, putting your code inside of it:

```
try {
    // your code goes here
}
```

Then, when your code runs, if it encounters an error, it is "thrown" as an exception. An exception is another name for an error. But instead of the program crashing, it will look for a `catch` clause to "catch" the exception. Start with the `catch` statement and another code block. After the `catch` statement, you need to indicate which type of exception it is looking to catch. The generic type is simply called `Exception`. Like a method, you need to give it a name you can refer to in the code block:

```
try {
    // your code goes here
} catch (Exception e) {
    // this code will run if an exception is caught
}
```

© Doug Winnie 2021
D. Winnie, *Essential Java for AP CompSci*, https://doi.org/10.1007/978-1-4842-6183-5_34

In the `catch` code block, you can then do things if an exception is thrown. For example, you can take the exception and display on the screen as a string:

```
try {
    // your code goes here
} catch (Exception e) {
    String error = e.toString();
    System.out.println(error);
}
```

"Catching" Specific Errors

You can also catch specific types of exceptions using a chain of `catch` statements. When the exception type matches a `catch` statement, it runs the code in the `catch` code block and skips the rest of them. In this example, if the type of exception is an `InputMismatchException`, the first catch block runs, but the second is skipped. When you add in the code for the specific type of exception, the IDE will automatically import it at the top of your code so you can work with it.

```
// at the top of the code
import java.util.InputMismatchException;

try {
    // your code goes here
} catch (InputMismatchException e) {
    System.out.println("You input the wrong type.");
} catch (Exception e) {
    String error = e.toString();
    System.out.println(error);
}
```

If you want to run something every time after a `try` block, regardless if an exception is thrown and caught, you can add a `finally` code block at the end that will run after a catch code block runs.

```
try {
    // your code goes here
} catch (InputMismatchException e) {
```

```
    System.out.println("You input the wrong type.");
} catch (Exception e) {
    String error = e.toString();
    System.out.println(error);
} finally {
    System.out.println("Thank you!");
}
```

Code Examples

The next page shows examples of capturing input from the user.

    This code is also available in the following GitHub repo:

```
https://github.com/Apress/essential-java-AP-CompSci
```

Listing 34-1. Catching errors

```java
import java.util.InputMismatchException;
import java.util.Scanner;

public class Main {

    // create an instance of the Scanner class
    public static Scanner sc;

    public static void main(String[] args) {
        // create the instance of the Scanner and
        // give it a name
        sc = new Scanner(System.in);
        System.out.print("Enter an integer value: ");

        // The try statement and the braces after it start a
        // code block that Java will attempt to run. It is a
        // safe area to run code and any errors that happen
        // will be captured.
        try {
            int intValue = sc.nextInt();
            System.out.printf("You entered %d.\n",intValue);
```

```java
} catch (Exception e) {
    // The catch statement and the code block after it
    // run when there is an error, also known as an
    // Exception. An exception can be of many types,
    // but when one is encountered, it is "thown" and
    // the catch statement catches it. If there are no
    // errors, the code in the catch block doesn't run.
    System.out.println("There was an error. Here is more info...");
    // The e variable that is part of the catch statement
    // contains information about the type of error. It is
    // the exception that is "caught" by the catch statement.
    // You can use the toString() method to display the
    // details of the error.
    System.out.println(e.toString());
}

// You can also capture specific exceptions. You can put multiple
// catch statements with different exception types. If an error
// is thrown, Java will run through the various catch statements
// until it finds one that matches the type. Then it will run through
// that and skip the rest of the catch statements.
sc = new Scanner(System.in);
System.out.print("Enter a short value (must be between -32,768 and
32,767): ");

try {
    short shortValue = sc.nextShort();
    System.out.printf("You entered %d.\n", shortValue);
} catch (InputMismatchException e) {
    System.out.println("The value is the wrong type. Maybe it is
    too big or small?");
} catch (Exception e) {
    System.out.println("There was an error. Here is more info...");
    System.out.println(e.toString());
} finally {
```

```
        // If you want to run code after a try block regardless if an
            error is caught,
        // you can add a finally statement and code block.
        System.out.println("Thank you for your answer!");
    }
  }
}

/* Output

Enter an integer value: 4.3
There was an error. Here is more info...
java.util.InputMismatchException
Enter a short value (must be between -32,768 and 32,767): 64000
The value is the wrong type. Maybe it is too big or small?
Thank you for your answer!

*/
```

Documenting with JavaDoc

Only part of being a software developer or engineer is about building code. A large portion of your role is to build documentation to support your other developers and potentially external developers who use your code to use it correctly.

To assist with this task, a tool called JavaDoc allows you as a developer to create specially coded comments to hold documentation around specific methods and components of your code.

Using JavaDoc Syntax

JavaDoc uses unique codes to denote sections of code that are parsed by the JavaDoc builder to create HTML documents for your code. When you update your code, you should rerun JavaDoc to ensure that your documentation is up to date. The following is an example of code that uses JavaDoc:

```
/** The Main class defines the entire project
 *
 * @author Doug Winnie
 * @version 1.0
 */

public class Main {

    /** integer variable that is used for calculations **/
    public static int val;
```

© Doug Winnie 2021
D. Winnie, *Essential Java for AP CompSci*, https://doi.org/10.1007/978-1-4842-6183-5_35

```
/**
 * The main method executes automatically when the program launches
 * @param args [Not used] Holds launch arguments for the program
 */
public static void main(String[] args) {
    val = 5;
    multiply(347, val);

}

/**
 * Calculates the product of two integers
 * @param a Integer for the first multiplier
 * @param b Integer for the second multiplyer
 * @return Integer value of the product of a and b
 */
public static int multiply(int a, int b)
{
    return a*b;
}
}
```

At the top is the documentation for your class, in this case, the Main class. A JavaDoc comment starts with /** vs. the normal /*.

The @author and @version tags are used to define the coder and version number of the program.

In the Main class, you create a description for each value member of the class using a /** */ comment before each member.

For a method, you create a /** */ comment, and the first line is the description of the method. Then each parameter is denoted using the @param tag, followed by the parameter name and then the description.

If a method returns a value, use the @return tag and then provide a description of what it returns.

IntelliJ will assist with the completion of JavaDoc comments after you complete the method. To do this, create your method, and then before it, start with the /** comment starting tag and press enter. It will create the comment framework, and then you can complete all of the sections.

Generating Documentation

When you create your code with JavaDoc, IntelliJ will highlight several of the items in your code and will also autocomplete some sections when you begin typing them.

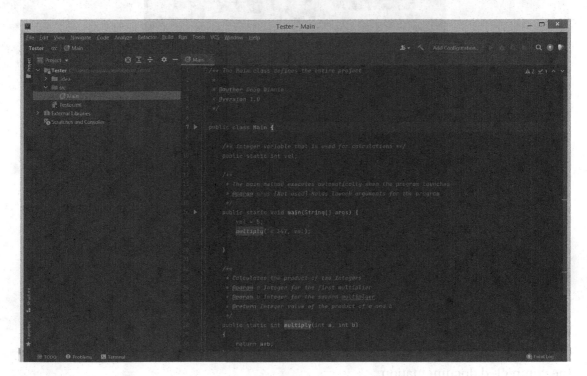

Figure 35-1. *Code using JavaDoc markup*

To build the JavaDoc, use the Tools ➤ Generate JavaDoc menu command.

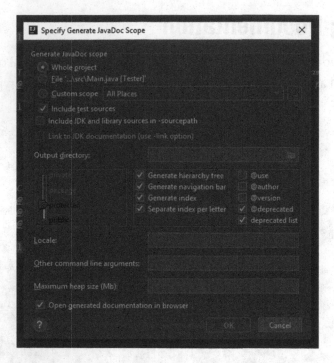

Figure 35-2. *JavaDoc window*

Check the @author and @version and define a location for where you want to save the generated HTML.

When you generate the documentation, it will open a browser window and show you the completed documentation.

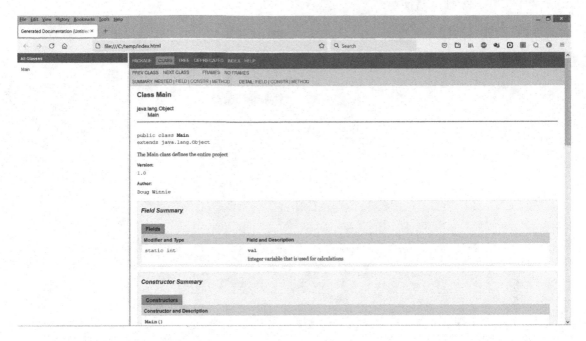

Figure 35-3. *Exported JavaDocs*

Code Examples

The preceding code is also available in the following GitHub repo:

https://github.com/Apress/essential-java-AP-CompSci

Formatted Strings

Previously, we have used the `printf()` method to create and output strings using formatters. Sometimes, you want to simply store the formatted string and not display it using a `String` variable.

You can do that using the `format()` method of the `String` class.

Creating a Formatted String Literal

To create a string literal, use the `String.format()` method. Inside, you place the string template along with the insertion codes and follow it with a comma-delimited list of the respective values to insert into the template. It is the same code you would use for the `printf()` method, but the result is a complete string:

```
String x = String.format("a: %s, b: %d, c: %.3f", a, b, c);
```

The result is the following string, assigned to x:

```
"a: foo, b: 5, c: 1.250"
```

Code Examples

The next page shows examples of creating a string literal with formatting.

This code is also available in the following GitHub repo:

```
https://github.com/Apress/essential-java-AP-CompSci
```

```
public class Main {

    public static void main(String[] args) {

        String a = "foo";
```

© Doug Winnie 2021
D. Winnie, *Essential Java for AP CompSci*, https://doi.org/10.1007/978-1-4842-6183-5_36

```
        int b = 5;
        double c = 1.25;

        String x = String.format("a: %s, b: %d, c: %.3f", a, b, c);

        System.out.println(x);

    }
}
```

The while Loop

Loops allow blocks of code to run repeatedly based on a condition. The most basic loop is called the while loop. The loop starts with the while statement and is followed by a condition, defined using an evaluation or expression that results in a Boolean answer of true or false.

If the result of the condition is true, the code within the loop executes, and the flow of the program returns to the top where it tests the condition again.

One issue with the while loop to consider is creating an infinite loop. This is when a loop will run forever because the condition at the top is always true. These will cause a runtime error and will cause your program to crash.

Create a while Loop

In the following code, a while loop is created using the while statement and is followed by a conditional evaluation. The evaluation tests if the variable val is less than 10. The variable is initialized with the integer literal value, 0.

```java
public class Main {

    public static void main(String[] args) {
        // This loop will run as long as the condition at the top
        // is always true

        int val = 0;

        while (val < 10) {
            System.out.println(String.format("val = %d",val));
            val++;
        }
```

© Doug Winnie 2021
D. Winnie, *Essential Java for AP CompSci*, https://doi.org/10.1007/978-1-4842-6183-5_37

```
        /* Output
        val = 0
        val = 1
        val = 2
        val = 3
        val = 4
        val = 5
        val = 6
        val = 7
        val = 8
        val = 9
        */

    }
}
```

The loop first tests the condition, which is true, because 0 is less than 10. Since the condition is true, it runs all of the code within the code block after the while statement.

At the end of the block, it increases the value stored in val, which is now 1, and repeats the loop.

Since the value stored in val is still less than 10, the loop runs again.

This continues until val is equal to 9. At the end of that execution of the loop, val is increased by 1 to equal 10. When the loop repeats this time, the condition at the top is now false, since 10 is not less than 10. With the condition now false, the loop ends, and the code block is skipped and the flow of the program continues.

Code Examples

The preceding code is also available in the following GitHub repo:

```
https://github.com/Apress/essential-java-AP-CompSci
```

SPRINT 38

Automatic Program Loops

Sometimes, you need to have a program loop continuously to complete certain tasks. You need to end the loop based on some condition, even if that condition is for the user to simply say to end the program using a command or action.

This is very common for games, where games will run and process logic, scenarios, and turns until a player wins, loses, or the user opts to end the game.

Creating a Program Loop

In the following example, a Boolean value called loopProgram is used to store a true or false value. The while loop runs until the Boolean is equal to false, which happens when the user enters the command "exit".

When that happens, the Boolean variable loopProgram is set to false, and the while loop then ends, and the program terminates.

Listing 38-1. Automatic program loop

```java
import java.util.Scanner;

public class Main {

    public static Scanner sc;
    public static boolean loopProgram;

    public static void main(String[] args) {
            sc = new Scanner(System.in);
            loopProgram = true;

            displayMenu();
```

183

© Doug Winnie 2021
D. Winnie, *Essential Java for AP CompSci*, https://doi.org/10.1007/978-1-4842-6183-5_38

```java
            while (loopProgram) {
                System.out.print("Command? ");
                String cmd = sc.next();
                parseCmd(cmd);
            }
    }

    public static void displayMenu() {
        System.out.println("Menu: ");
        System.out.println("north: move north ");
        System.out.println("south: move south ");
        System.out.println(" east: move east ");
        System.out.println(" west: move west ");
        System.out.println(" exit: quit program ");
    }

    public static void parseCmd(String cmd) {
        switch (cmd) {
            case "north":
                System.out.println("You move north.");
                break;
            case "south":
                System.out.println("You move south.");
                break;
            case "east":
                System.out.println("You move east.");
                break;
            case "west":
                System.out.println("You move west.");
                break;
            case "exit":
                System.out.println("Goodbye");
                loopProgram = false;
                break;
```

```
        default:
            System.out.println("Unrecognized command!");
            break;
        }
    }
}
```

Code Examples

The preceding code is also available in the following GitHub repo:

https://github.com/Apress/essential-java-AP-CompSci

The do/while Loop

The while loop runs if the condition at the top is true, but you might have a case when you need to run the code in the loop at least once, or you need to test the condition at the end of the loop.

The solution to this is the do...while loop. The do...while loop is identical to the while loop, except the condition statement is tested at the end. As a result, the loop will always run at least one time, and if the condition at the end of the loop is true, the loop will repeat. If the condition at the end is false, it will not repeat the loop, and the flow of the program will continue with the next statement.

Creating a do...while Loop

A do...while loop starts with the do clause and then a code block, defined by braces. After the code block, the while clause is added with the conditional statement:

```
int a = 5;
do {
System.out.println(a);
a--;
} while (a > 0);
```

In this example, the loop will run five times, starting with the value 5 and then decrement that by 1 with each execution of the loop.

© Doug Winnie 2021
D. Winnie, *Essential Java for AP CompSci*, https://doi.org/10.1007/978-1-4842-6183-5_39

Run at Least Once

In the following example, the loop will run once, because the condition is tested at the end:

```
boolean loop = false;
```

```
do {
System.out.println("Run this loop!");
} while (loop);
```

Simplified Assignment Operators

There are a number of shortcuts you can use to manipulate the value of a variable to save time. These are called combined assignment operators, where they perform a mathematical evaluation on the existing value of a variable and assign the result back to the same variable.

Combined Assignment

Take this code, for instance:

```
int a = 2;
System.out.println(a);

a = a + 2;
System.out.println(a);
```

In this example, we have an integer variable called a that is set to the literal value 2. Then we take the value stored in the variable, and we perform addition to increase the value by 2. We take that new result, 4, and assign this back to a.

We can simplify this using the following statement:

```
a += 2;
```

This performs the same action as the previous statement but does so more concisely.

© Doug Winnie 2021
D. Winnie, *Essential Java for AP CompSci*, https://doi.org/10.1007/978-1-4842-6183-5_40

You can use this combined assignment operator with all basic arithmetic operators including addition, subtraction, multiplication, division, and modulo:

```
a += 2;
a -= 2;
a *= 2;
a /= 2;
a %= 2;
```

Increment and Decrement

If you only want to add or subtract one, there are two additional shortcuts. The first is the increment operator. To add one to any variable, add a double plus at the end of the variable:

```
a = a + 1;
a += 1;
a++;
```

All three of these statements do the same thing: add one to the value stored in the variable a. The last one uses the increment operator.

To subtract one, just replace the plus signs with minus signs:

```
a = a - 1;
a -= 1;
a--;
```

Placement and Program Flow

When you use operators like these, you can use them to change values and display values at the same time.

Let's look at this example:

```
int a = 1;
System.out.println(a);        // 1
System.out.println(a += 1); // 2
System.out.println(a);        // 2
```

When we use the combined assignment operator in this scenario, we are using it to display the value of a, while at the same time alter the value. The math is performed first, and then the value is displayed.

Let's change this to use the increment operator:

```
int b = 1;
System.out.println(b);        // 1
System.out.println(b++);      // 1
System.out.println(b);        // 2
```

When we run this one, something unexpected happens. Even though we are adding one to the value using the increment operator, it isn't displaying it. When we redisplay the value, the new increased value displays.

So, the value is being increased, but it is happening after the value is displayed. That is the order the code runs when the increment operator is placed after the variable name.

We can resolve this by placing the operator before the variable name as a prefix:

```
int c = 1;
System.out.println(c);        // 1
System.out.println(++c);      // 2
System.out.println(c);        // 2
```

Depending on the needs of your program, you may need to place the operator before or after the variable. Most scenarios will have you place it after it, but using it as a prefix can be valuable in some circumstances.

Code Examples

The next page shows examples of simplified assignment operators.

This code is also available in the following GitHub repo:

```
https://github.com/Apress/essential-java-AP-CompSci
```

Listing 40-1. Simplified assignment operator examples

```
public class Main {

    public static void main(String[] args) {

        int x = 10;

        System.out.println("Combined assignment");

        x += 5;      // 15
        System.out.println(x);

        x -= 5;      // 10
        System.out.println(x);

        x *= 2;      // 20
        System.out.println(x);

        x /= 4;      // 5
        System.out.println(x);

        x %= 2;      // 1
        System.out.println(x);

        System.out.println("\nInline combined assignment");

        int a = 1;
        System.out.println(a);        // 1
        System.out.println(a += 1); // 2
        System.out.println(a);        // 2

        System.out.println("\nPost increment");

        int b = 1;
        System.out.println(b);        // 1
        System.out.println(b++);      // 1
        System.out.println(b);        // 2

        System.out.println("\nPre increment");
```

```java
        int c = 1;
        System.out.println(c);        // 1
        System.out.println(++c);      // 2
        System.out.println(c);        // 2
    }
}
```

The for Loop

The for loop runs for a specific number of times, based on a special variable called the iterator. The iterator's value, conditional test result, and modifications for each execution of the loop (called the step) controls the runtime of the loop. All three of these items are defined at the beginning of the for loop.

A for loop is used when you need to repeat a sequence a specific number of times. For instance, if you need to run through the same code a hundred times or based on some specific, fixed number of times.

Creating a for Loop

The for loop starts with the for clause and then contains a pair of parentheses. Inside the parentheses, separated by a semicolon, three items are set up:

1. The type and variable name used for the iterator value for the loop, with an initial value assigned

2. The conditional test that will need to be true for the loop to run

3. The modification made to the iterator at the end of the for loop

Here is an example of a loop that will run ten times:

```
for (int i = 0; i < 10; i++) {
    System.out.println(i);
}
```

In this example, we have an iterator variable, called i, that is typed as an integer and is initially set to the integer literal value of 0. We then define the for loop to run only if the iterator is less than ten. Then at the end of the loop, the iterator increases by one using the increment operator.

© Doug Winnie 2021
D. Winnie, *Essential Java for AP CompSci*, https://doi.org/10.1007/978-1-4842-6183-5_41

When you run this loop, you get the following output:

```
0
1
2
3
4
5
6
7
8
9
```

The iterator is 0 for the start of the loop, and the condition passes, so the loop runs. At the end of the loop, it increments the iterator to 1 and repeats the conditional test, which passes again, and the loop runs again.

This continues until the iterator is equal to 9. At the end of that execution of the loop, the iterator increments to 10, repeats the conditional test, which this time fails, and the flow of the program continues past the loop.

Changing the Step

You can modify the step to be whatever you need it to be to meet the needs of your program. For instance, you can loop through all of the even numbers from 2 to 100:

```java
for (int i = 2; i <= 100; i=i+2) {
    System.out.println(i);
}
```

Inside the loop, we can use the repetitions to run code, for instance, we can test the probability of getting a head, 0, or a tail, 1, and see if it matches the probability formula:

```java
int timesTrue = 0;
int timesFalse = 0;
int timesRun = 1000000;
```

```java
for (int i = 0; i <= timesRun; i++) {
    int result = (int)Math.round(Math.random());
    System.out.println(String.format("Attempt %d: %d", i, result));
    if (result == 0)
    {
        timesTrue++;
    } else {
        timesFalse++;
    }
}

float perTrue = (float) timesTrue / (float) timesRun * 100;
float perFalse = (float) timesFalse / (float) timesRun * 100;

System.out.println(String.format("Out of %d tests,",timesRun));
System.out.println(String.format("Times true : %d, or %.2f",timesTrue,
perTrue) + "%");
System.out.println(String.format("Times false: %d, or %.2f",timesFalse,
perFalse) + "%");
```

Code Examples

The preceding code is also available in the following GitHub repo:

```
https://github.com/Apress/essential-java-AP-CompSci
```

Nesting Loops

When you create a `for` loop, what's stopping you from creating two? Nothing! In fact, it is very common to create nested for loops that run inside of one another. A nested `for` loop is when two (or more) loops run inside of one another.

Creating Nested Loops

If we start with a basic loop, we can count from the numbers zero through nine.

```
for (int i = 0; i < 10; i++) {
    System.out.println(i);
}
```

But then we can create another loop inside of this one that will count zero through nine again.

```
for (int i = 0; i < 10; i++) {
    for (int j = 0; j < 10; j++) {
        System.out.printf("(%d,%d)\n",i,j);
    }
}
```

There are a few important rules to note here. The first is that the loops are entirely encapsulated within the other. You can't have loops overlap; they must fit entirely within another loop.

The other is that the iterator variable needs to be unique for the two loops. The outer loop uses the iterator variable `i`. The inner loop uses the variable `j` as the iterator. The rules for scope apply here, because inside the inner loop, I can access the `i` and `j` variables, but in the outer loop, I can only access the `i` variable since the inner loop is out of scope outside of it.

© Doug Winnie 2021
D. Winnie, *Essential Java for AP CompSci*, https://doi.org/10.1007/978-1-4842-6183-5_42

The code inside the inner loop is able to access both iterator variables and outputs text to the console:

```
(0,0)
(0,1)
(0,2)
(0,3)
(0,4)
(0,5)
(0,6)
(0,7)
(0,8)
(0,9)
(1,0)
(1,1)
(1,2)
. . .
(9,3)
(9,4)
(9,5)
(9,6)
(9,7)
(9,8)
(9,9)
```

The first number is the outer loop, or i. The second number is the inner loop, or j. As you can see, they resemble the coordinates on a grid. You can think of a nested loop as a way to systematically go through the coordinates or cells of a grid, starting with the rows (i) and columns (j).

Displaying as a Grid

We can use that to help build grids of information, like a multiplication table. Following the flow of the nested loop structure, we can create output using the print() method to add to the display with each execution of the inner loop, and then create new rows with each start of the outer loop.

Here is an example, using the \t sequence to denote a tab space in the output to keep things lined up:

```
System.out.println("Building a grid:");
System.out.println("\t0:\t1:\t2:\t3:\t4:\t5:\t6:\t7:\t8:\t9:");
for (int i = 0; i < 10; i++) {
    System.out.printf("%d:\t",i);
    for (int j = 0; j < 10; j++) {
        System.out.printf("%d\t",i*j);
    }
    System.out.print("\n");
}
```

When this loop runs, it starts with a heading and then creates a list of column headers, then it enters into the outer loop, counting from zero to ten. It starts by printing the row header but doesn't go to the next line. Then the inner loop runs, also counting from zero to ten. It adds a little bit of text to the end of the current line of text on the screen, displaying the product of i and j, followed by a tab space. Then after the inner loop runs out, it adds a newline character to the end of the text on the screen and repeats the loop again for another row.

The result from this is the following:

```
Building a grid:
        0:   1:   2:   3:   4:   5:   6:   7:   8:   9:
0:      0    0    0    0    0    0    0    0    0    0
1:      0    1    2    3    4    5    6    7    8    9
2:      0    2    4    6    8    10   12   14   16   18
3:      0    3    6    9    12   15   18   21   24   27
4:      0    4    8    12   16   20   24   28   32   36
5:      0    5    10   15   20   25   30   35   40   45
6:      0    6    12   18   24   30   36   42   48   54
7:      0    7    14   21   28   35   42   49   56   63
8:      0    8    16   24   32   40   48   56   64   72
9:      0    9    18   27   36   45   54   63   72   81
```

Code Examples

The preceding example code is listed in the following in a complete program file.

This code is also available on GitHub at this location:

https://github.com/Apress/essential-java-AP-CompSci

Listing 42-1. Nested loop examples

```java
public class Main {

    public static void main(String[] args) {

        // Single loop
        System.out.println("Single loop");

        for (int i = 0; i < 10; i++) {
            System.out.println(i);
        }

        // Nested loop
        System.out.println("\nNested loop");

        for (int i = 0; i < 10; i++) {
            for (int j = 0; j < 10; j++) {
                System.out.printf("(%d,%d)\n",i,j);
            }
        }

        // Building a grid
        System.out.println("\nBuilding a grid:");
        System.out.println("\t0:\t1:\t2:\t3:\t4:\t5:\t6:\t7:\t8:\t9:");
        for (int i = 0; i < 10; i++) {
            System.out.printf("%d:\t",i);
            for (int j = 0; j < 10; j++) {
                System.out.printf("%d\t",i*j);
            }
            System.out.print("\n");
        }
    }
}
```

Strings as Collections

Strings are much more robust than they appear to be. They have several properties and capabilities that you can use methods to unlock to manipulate and manage contents of strings. These include finding the length of the string, extracting a specific character from a string, comparing strings, and pulling out a substring out of a larger string.

Creating Strings Using the String Class

Creating a string requires using the String class. Because we are using a class vs. a primitive as the type, we need to use the new keyword for the string:

```
String s = new String();
s = "Doug";
```

Getting a String Length

Strings have a method called length() that returns an integer containing the number of characters in the string:

```
// Getting the length of a string
int len = s.length();
System.out.println(len); // Returns 4
```

Getting a Specific Character from a String

Strings are indexed based on the characters that are within them. They use a counting number sequence starting with zero to identify each number. Using the charAt() method, you can extract the specific character at an index location within the string:

© Doug Winnie 2021
D. Winnie, *Essential Java for AP CompSci*, https://doi.org/10.1007/978-1-4842-6183-5_43

```
// Getting the first character of a string
char firstLetter = s.charAt(0);
System.out.println(firstLetter); // Returns D
```

Finding a Character in a String

When you have a string, there are times you need to find a specific character, for instance, if you have a string containing someone's full name, you might need to find the location of a space or special character in it.

To do this, you can use the indexOf() method of the String class and provide it a character, or a string, that it will attempt to find in the string:

```
String name = "Doug Winnie";
int space = name.indexOf(" ");
System.out.println(space); // Outputs 4
```

This will find the first instance of the character in the string. If you need to find more than one, you can use an overloaded version of the indexOf() method that provides a specific starting location for your search:

```
String state = "Mississippi";
int start = 0;
boolean loop = true;

do {
    int index = state.indexOf('i',start);
    System.out.println(index);
    if (index >= 0) {
        start = index + 1;
    } else {
        loop = false;
    }
} while (loop); // Program outputs 1, 4, 7, 10, -1
```

In the preceding example, we have an integer that contains where we want to start the search, using a character location number, then a boolean to control the execution of the loop.

When we run the indexOf() method, we pass in the character literal we want to find and the location where we want to start the search. When it finds a value, it assigns that to the index integer variable. If it doesn't find the character, it assigns the value -1, meaning that the sequence cannot be found.

If it finds the value, it then updates the start search index, or if it can't find any more of the value, it sets up the loop to end.

Finally, you can look for the last instance of a character in a string using the lastIndexOf() method:

```
String name = "Doug Winnie";
int ichar = name.lastIndexOf('i');
System.out.println(ichar); // Outputs 9
```

Extracting a Substring

To capture a section of a string within a larger string, you can use the substring() method. There are two overloaded method options. The first is to provide the index number of where you want to start the substring to extract. The second is to provide the start and end index point of the string that you want to capture within the larger string:

```
// Getting a substring from the end
String sub = s.substring(1);
System.out.println(sub); // Returns oug

// Getting a substring from the middle
String mid = s.substring(1,3);
System.out.println(mid); // Returns ou
```

Comparing Strings

To compare strings, use the equals() method. Due to the nature of reference types, it is best to use the equals() method to compare strings vs. the equality operator (==):

```
// Comparing a string
boolean isSame = s.equals("Doug");
System.out.println(isSame); // Returns true
```

Another helpful comparison tool is the equalsIgnoreCase() method. This compares the contents of two strings and returns true regardless of whether the cases match between the two. So, the strings "Abc", "abc", and "ABC" would result in true if compared using the equalsIgnoreCase() method:

```
isSame = s.equals("DOUG");
System.out.println(isSame); // Returns false

isSame = s.equalsIgnoreCase("DOUG");
System.out.println(isSame); // Returns true
```

Code Examples

The following code contains examples of working with strings and how to use string methods.

This code is also available at GitHub at the following location:

```
https://github.com/Apress/essential-java-AP-CompSci
```

Listing 43-1. String method examples

```
public class Main {

    public static void main(String[] args) {

        // Creating a string
        String s = new String();
        s = "Doug";

        // Getting the length of a string
        int len = s.length();
        System.out.println(len); // Returns 4

        // Getting the first character of a string
        char firstLetter = s.charAt(0);
        System.out.println(firstLetter); // Returns D
```

```
// Get location of specific string or character
String name = "Doug Winnie";
int space = name.indexOf(" ");
System.out.println(space);

// Get location of specific string or character from a custom start
point
String state = "Mississippi";
int start = 0;
boolean loop = true;

do {
    int index = state.indexOf('i',start);
    System.out.println(index);
    if (index >= 0) {
        start = index + 1;
    } else {
        loop = false;
    }
} while (loop);
// Get the last location of a specific string or character
name = "Doug Winnie";
int ichar = name.lastIndexOf('i');
System.out.println(ichar);

// Getting a substring from the end
String sub = s.substring(1);
System.out.println(sub); // Returns oug

// Getting a substring from the middle
String mid = s.substring(1,3);
System.out.println(mid); // Returns ou

// Comparing a string
boolean isSame = s.equals("Doug");
System.out.println(isSame); // Returns true
```

```
        isSame = s.equals("DOUG");
        System.out.println(isSame); // Returns false

        isSame = s.equalsIgnoreCase("DOUG");
        System.out.println(isSame); // Returns true
    }
}
```

Make Collections Using Arrays

Arrays are collections of identically typed objects that you can refer to as a single name. You can also access the individual items within them using bracket notation and using index numbers.

Creating an Array with Values

Arrays are defined just like any other variable. You need to define the type of values that will be contained within the array and use a pair of brackets to indicate that you are creating an array instead of a single value.

There are two ways you can create an array. You can create an array from a set of values, or you can define an empty array by declaring how many elements will be contained inside of it. The key thing to know is that an array must be defined with a specific number of items in order to create it. You cannot change the number of items in the array after it is created.

To create an array from a set of values, start with the type of value that will be stored in the array, followed by a pair of square brackets. Then use the assignment operator and create a new array using the new statement, followed by the array value type and another pair of square brackets. Then follow with a set of values that match the array type, encapsulated in braces and separated by commas:

```
// Creating an array from values
int[] a = new int[] {1,2,3,4,5};
```

This array, called a, can only contain integers since it is typed as an int. Since we provided a value immediately, the array will contain five values, and they are initially 1, 2, 3, 4, and 5.

209

© Doug Winnie 2021

D. Winnie, *Essential Java for AP CompSci*, https://doi.org/10.1007/978-1-4842-6183-5_44

Getting a Value from an Array

To access a value in an array, you need to use the brackets to indicate which element you want to get, using an index number. Remember, the first element in an array is index number 0:

```
// Accessing values in an array
System.out.println(a[0]); // Outputs 1
```

Creating an Array by Size

Alternatively, you can create an array by defining the size of it and provide the values later. The structure is generally the same, but you provide the size inside the square brackets and omit the list of values:

```
// Creating an array by size
int[] b = new int[5];
```

This array is empty but can contain five values inside of it. To add values to these five slots, you can access the array, specify an index element, and then assign a value into it using the assignment operator:

```
// Assigning values to an array
b[0] = 5;
```

Things to Avoid with Arrays

There are a few potential pitfalls you should know when you work with arrays. The first is when you define an empty array by defining the size, Java automatically assigns a value to each element, even if you don't provide one. This can lead to unexpected results, so it is recommended that you don't keep an array empty for long.

Another common error is to access elements of an array that don't exist by providing an invalid index number.

Finally, since arrays are typed to a value, all of the elements of the array must match the value defined when it was first created:

```
// Errors with arrays
// System.out.println(b[1]); // Returns a 0 since no value was assigned
// b[5] = 9; // No index 5 exists
// int[] c = new int[] {1.2,3.4,5.6}; // Doesn't match type
// int[] d = new int[] {1,2,3,4.5}; // Mixed types
```

Getting the Number of Values in an Array

Just like with strings, you can find out the number of items within the array. With a string, you could find the number of characters. With arrays, you can find the number of elements. The difference is that you access the length using a property, not a method, so you need to omit the pair of parentheses at the end:

```
// Getting the array length
int len = a.length;
System.out.println(len); // Returns 5
```

Looping Through an Array

Finally, you can loop through the elements of an array, just like the characters of a string. By using the element index number, bracket notation, and the length property, you can loop through all the elements.

The following code shows how you can create an array based on several elements defined by the user and then populate those values using a loop:

```
// Defining an array using input
Scanner sc = new Scanner(System.in);

System.out.print("How many numbers do you want to add? ");
int count = sc.nextInt();

int[] values = new int[count];
```

```java
for (int i = 0; i < values.length; i++)
{
    System.out.printf("Value %d: ", i);
    int num = sc.nextInt();

    values[i] = num;
}

int sum = 0;
for (int i = 0; i < values.length; i++)
{
    sum += values[i];
}

System.out.printf("Sum: %d\n", sum);
```

Code Examples

This code is also available on GitHub at the following location:

https://github.com/Apress/essential-java-AP-CompSci

Listing 44-1. Array examples

```java
import java.util.Scanner;

public class Main {

    public static void main(String[] args) {
        // Creating an array from values
        int[] a = new int[] {1,2,3,4,5};

        // Accessing values in an array
        System.out.println(a[0]);

        // Creating an array by size
        int[] b = new int[5];

        // Assigning values to an array
        b[0] = 5;
```

```
// Errors with arrays
// System.out.println(b[1]); // Returns a 0 since no value was assigned
// b[5] = 9; // No index 5 exists
// int[] c = new int[] {1.2,3.4,5.6}; // Doesn't match type
// int[] d = new int[] {1,2,3,4.5}; // Mixed types

// Getting the array length
int len = a.length;
System.out.println(len);

// Looping through an array
for (int i = 0; i < a.length; i++)
{
    System.out.printf("Index %d: %d\n",i, a[i]);
}

// Defining an array using input
Scanner sc = new Scanner(System.in);

System.out.print("How many numbers do you want to add? ");
int count = sc.nextInt();

int[] values = new int[count];

for (int i = 0; i < values.length; i++)
{
    System.out.printf("Value %d: ", i);
    int num = sc.nextInt();

    values[i] = num;
}

int sum = 0;
for (int i = 0; i < values.length; i++)
{
    sum += values[i];
}

System.out.printf("Sum: %d\n", sum);
    }
}
```

Creating Arrays from Strings

Often, you will work with data that has been formatted or analyzed before you use it in your program. One of the common ways to send and transmit information is using a delimited list.

A delimited list is a simple list of items that are separated by a delimiter. This could be a comma, a pipe (or vertical bar), a semicolon, tab, space, or any character that you see fit. In Java, you can work with delimited lists that are stored as `Strings` and then parse them into `Arrays` using the `split()` method.

Delimited Strings

To start, you need to have a string that contains a delimited list. The delimiter needs to be the same throughout the string and needs to be unique and only used as a delimiter. Here is an example:

```
String list = "Doug,Mike,Janet,Matt,Tim,Doris";
```

This string will work because the comma is the delimiter. This list contains six unique items that are names, but are stored in a string, with the comma indicating when one item ends and another begins.

We might have an issue though if the string looked like this:

```
String list = "Doug, Mike, Janet, Matt, Tim, Doris";
```

The difference is subtle, but between the names isn't only a comma, but a comma and a space. If we break these up into multiple items based on the comma, we would have five items that would have a space before them.

© Doug Winnie 2021
D. Winnie, *Essential Java for AP CompSci*, https://doi.org/10.1007/978-1-4842-6183-5_45

Splitting It Up

To create an array using a delimited list, we need to use the split() method and provide the delimiter that is used in the string. The result will be a string-typed array containing all the items in the string within unique elements:

```
String list = "Doug,Mike,Janet,Matt,Tim,Doris";
String[] names = list.split(",");
```

When this code runs, the string with the names will be parsed using the split() method and will split it whenever it finds a comma. The collection of split strings is then sequentially added to the string-typed array names. The original list remains unchanged.

We can then display the individual names using element index numbers or loop through the collection to see all the values that were parsed:

```
System.out.printf("List: %s\n\n", list);

System.out.printf("Item 2: %s\n\n",names[2]);

for (var i = 0; i < names.length; i++)
    System.out.printf("Name %d: %s\n",i,names[i]);
```

The preceding code will display the original list, a single item from the new array that was created, and then loop through and display all the names in the list:

```
List: Doug,Mike,Janet,Matt,Tim,Doris

Item 2: Janet

Name 0: Doug
Name 1: Mike
Name 2: Janet
Name 3: Matt
Name 4: Tim
Name 5: Doris
```

What About Numbers?

This works great with strings, but if we have numbers, what do we do? We need to create the array of strings first and then create a new array and convert those values to numbers.

```
String nums = "3,6,9,12,15,18,21";
String strValues[] = nums.split(",");
int[] values = new int[strValues.length];

for (int i = 0; i < strValues.length; i++)
    values[i] = Integer.parseInt(strValues[i]);
```

Here, we have a string of integers, separated by commas. When we split these, the values are still strings, so we need to store them in a string-typed array.

Then, an empty integer-typed array is created with the same number of elements as the string-typed array. A for loop then loops through the string-typed array and parses each element string value into an integer and assigns it to the same element in the integer-typed array.

When this is finished, we now have a new integer array with the parsed values inside. We can display them using a for loop:

```
for (int i = 0; i < values.length; i++)
    System.out.printf("Value %d: %d\n",i,values[i]);
```

This will loop through all the values of the integer array, and we can work with them as integers in our program. The output for this is as follows:

```
Value 0: 3
Value 1: 6
Value 2: 9
Value 3: 12
Value 4: 15
Value 5: 18
Value 6: 21
```

Code Examples

This code is also available on GitHub at the following location:

https://github.com/Apress/essential-java-AP-CompSci

Listing 45-1. Parsing arrays from strings

```java
public class Main {

    public static void main(String[] args) {

        // Splitting a delimited string into an array

        String list = "Doug,Mike,Janet,Matt,Tim,Doris";
        String[] names = list.split(",");

        System.out.printf("List: %s\n\n", list);

        System.out.printf("Item 2: %s\n\n",names[2]);

        for (var i = 0; i < names.length; i++)
            System.out.printf("Name %d: %s\n",i,names[i]);

        // Splitting a delimited string into an integer array

        String nums = "3,6,9,12,15,18,21";
        String strValues[] = nums.split(",");
        int[] values = new int[strValues.length];

        for (int i = 0; i < strValues.length; i++)
            values[i] = Integer.parseInt(strValues[i]);

        for (int i = 0; i < values.length; i++)
            System.out.printf("Value %d: %d\n",i,values[i]);

    }
}
```

SPRINT 46

Multidimensional Arrays

A set is a collection of values. For arrays, these values are all the same type. If an array element can contain a value, can it store a set of values? The answer is yes.

An array can store almost anything if it is the same type as the other values. So, if an array can contain a collection of integers, it can just as easily store a collection of integer sets.

These are called multidimensional arrays. The name refers to the fact that the set can contain multiple dimensions of data. A single dimension would be a single row of data:

```
1,
2,
3,
4,
5,
```

A second dimension would convert each of those into a set of their own, creating a grid:

```
1,2,3,4,5,
2,3,4,5,6,
3,4,5,6,7,
4,5,6,7,8,
5,6,7,8,9
```

You could even take this a bit further and give each cell of this grid a set of their own, creating a three-dimensional cube of data.

© Doug Winnie 2021

D. Winnie, *Essential Java for AP CompSci*, https://doi.org/10.1007/978-1-4842-6183-5_46

Define a Multidimensional Array

To define an array with multiple dimensions is no different than a simple array, but you need to say how many dimensions you are going to make.

Remember, when you define a variable, you are providing the type. If it is a simple integer, it is an `int`. If it is a collection of integers, it is an `int[]`. This `int[]` is the complete type. It isn't a representation or an abstraction; it is clearly stating that the only thing that the variable can hold is a collection of integers.

So for an array with multiple dimensions, the same thing applies:

```
int[] values;
int[][] grid;
```

The first variable, `values`, stores a single dimension of integers. To create a second dimension, we add another pair of empty brackets, like we use with the variable `grid`.

When you define the size of the array, but don't want to provide the values, you can do that using the `new` statement and with values inside the brackets, like this:

```
values = new int[5];
grid = new int[5][5];
```

Alternatively, you can use brace notation (sometimes referred to as object notation) and provide the values at the same time as initializing the array:

```
values = new int[] {1,2,3,4,5};
grid = new int[][] {{1,2,3,4,5},
                    {2,3,4,5,6},
                    {3,4,5,6,7},
                    {4,5,6,7,8},
                    {5,6,7,8,9}};
```

The whitespace for the `grid` variable was added to show what we have going on here; we essentially have a few rows of data that we are adding, one at a time.

This could alternatively be written like this:

```
grid = new int[][] {{1,2,3,4,5}, {2,3,4,5,6}, {3,4,5,6,7}, {4,5,6,7,8},
{5,6,7,8,9}};
```

Assign Values to Multidimensional Arrays

Assigning values to a specific element in a multidimensional array is no different than with a single dimension, except that you now need to provide multiple values for each dimension:

```
values[3] = 0;
grid[2][1] = 0;
```

Again, both the simple array and the multidimensional array are shown here for comparison.

Access Values in Multidimensional Arrays

Like with assigning values, you need to provide two element identification numbers to access an item in an array.

```
System.out.println("values element 3: " + values[3]);
System.out.println("grid element 2, element 4: " + grid[2][4]);
```

In addition, you can also access the first dimension only and then work with the items inside. This is done by only referring to the first dimension of the array.

```
System.out.println("values in element 1: " + grid[1].length);
```

Rectangular and Irregular Arrays

In the examples earlier, we have the same number of items in each dimension. Examples like this, where we could have five sets of five values, are called rectangular arrays. There is a consistent number of sets and values in the sets. While five sets of five values creates a square, this could also be three sets of eight values, or a hundred sets of two values—it doesn't matter, but the size of the sets is always consistent.

But they don't have to be; you could easily create an array like this:

```
int[][] irrGrid = new int[][] {{1,2},{3,4,5},{6,7,8,9}};
```

In this example, there are three sets, but there are a varying number of values within each of these sets. This is called an irregular sized array. The same rules apply though as they do for all arrays. When you create an array, you can't add elements, and you can't remove them. So the size of this array will always be irregular.

Code Examples

This code is also available on GitHub at the following location:

https://github.com/Apress/essential-java-AP-CompSci

Listing 46-1. Multidimensional arrays

```
public class Main {

    public static void main(String[] args) {

        int[] values;
        int[][] grid;

        // values = new int[5];
        // grid = new int[5][5];

        values = new int[] {1,2,3,4,5};
        grid = new int[][] {{1,2,3,4,5},
                            {2,3,4,5,6},
                            {3,4,5,6,7},
                            {4,5,6,7,8},
                            {5,6,7,8,9}};

        values[3] = 0;
        grid[2][1] = 0;

        System.out.println("values element 3: " + values[3]);
        System.out.println("grid element 2, element 4: " + grid[2][4]);

        System.out.println("values in element 1: " + grid[1].length);
    }
}
```

```
/* Output

values element 3: 0
grid element 2, element 4: 7
values in element 1: 5

*/
```

SPRINT 47

Looping Through Multidimensional Arrays

Using for loops with multidimensional arrays can be a bit tricky, but essentially they are the same as loops created with simple arrays; you just have to have a loop for each dimension nested within another.

Creating Nested Loops for Arrays

The following is an example of building a grid of data, generating that data, and displaying it on the screen. It is done using two loops.

First, we need to initialize our grid of data:

```
int[][] multitable = new int[10][10];
```

This array will contain ten sets of ten integers. It is initialized, but the values inside of each element are currently empty, or null. We need to create data to put inside of it.

We can build a multiplication table of data where the cell is equal to the product of the row and column. We can display the values on the screen and separate them with tab spaces to line them up.

A two-dimensional array consists of multiple rows, each containing individual items. When we create the loop, we need to loop through each row, and then when we are focused on a specific row, loop for each element or column within that row. So we need to create a two-level deep nested for loop. Instead of using the typical iterator variable names, we will use row and col to represent them.

225

© Doug Winnie 2021

D. Winnie, *Essential Java for AP CompSci*, https://doi.org/10.1007/978-1-4842-6183-5_47

First, let's create the values in the array:

```
for (int row = 0; row < multitable.length; row++) {
    for (int col = 0; col < multitable[row].length; col++) {
        multitable[row][col] = row*col;
    }
}
```

When we access the length property, we need to remember what we are finding the length of. On the first line, we need to find the number of rows or the first dimension of elements within the array. Then for the second line, where we start the second nested loop, we want to find the number of elements within a specific row, so we include the first set of brackets to indicate which set we are working with and then get the number of items.

Finally, we access a specific element and then set it to a value: the product of the row and col variables.

Systematically, the entire grid is created, starting with the first set and with its first value, then all of the values of the first set are generated. When the last value of the first set is created, the outer loop then goes to the second set, and the process starts over again.

When the last set wraps up, we now have a grid of data we can work with. We can then replicate the loops to display the values on the screen:

```
for (int row = 0; row < multitable.length; row++) {
    for (int col = 0; col < multitable[row].length; col++) {
        System.out.print(multitable[row][col] + "\t");
    }
    System.out.println();
}
```

The same thing happens here; we start with the first set and access each value within it. When it is displayed on the screen, a tab space is added to the end.

When the values for one set are finished, a new line is added before it repeats everything again for the next set.

The result is this:

0	0	0	0	0	0	0	0	0	0
0	1	2	3	4	5	6	7	8	9
0	2	4	6	8	10	12	14	16	18
0	3	6	9	12	15	18	21	24	27

0	4	8	12	16	20	24	28	32	36
0	5	10	15	20	25	30	35	40	45
0	6	12	18	24	30	36	42	48	54
0	7	14	21	28	35	42	49	56	63
0	8	16	24	32	40	48	56	64	72
0	9	18	27	36	45	54	63	72	81

Code Examples

This code is also available on GitHub at the following location:

https://github.com/Apress/essential-java-AP-CompSci

Listing 47-1. Loops for multidimensional arrays

```java
public class Main {

    public static void main(String[] args) {

        int[][] multitable = new int[10][10];

        for (int row = 0; row < multitable.length; row++) {
            for (int col = 0; col < multitable[row].length; col++) {
                multitable[row][col] = row*col;
            }
        }

        for (int row = 0; row < multitable.length; row++) {
            for (int col = 0; col < multitable[row].length; col++) {
                System.out.print(multitable[row][col] + "\t");
            }
            System.out.println();
        }
    }
}
```

227

Beyond Arrays with ArrayLists

Arrays are great at storing collections of values, but they have a lot of limitations. First, they can only hold items that are of the same type. Next, they have to be explicitly defined when they are created. Finally, they can't be resized after they are created.

To get around these limitations, there is a more flexible collection format known as the `ArrayList`. This type of collection can handle different types, and you can change the values and size of it after it is created.

The trade-off is that the `ArrayList` syntax is more complicated. The `ArrayList` is a Java class, so we will need to use methods to work with the properties and values within it.

Create an ArrayList

The `ArrayList` class isn't a default class that is part of a basic program, so we need to import the class into the program before we can use it. At the top of your code, you need to add this line:

```
import java.util.ArrayList;
```

Then, you can create an `ArrayList` by typing it to the class. Inside the constructor parentheses, you can optionally define how many values are in the `ArrayList`, but it isn't required:

```
ArrayList names = new ArrayList();
```

© Doug Winnie 2021
D. Winnie, *Essential Java for AP CompSci*, https://doi.org/10.1007/978-1-4842-6183-5_48

Add Items to ArrayLists

Adding an element into an ArrayList is done using the add() method:

```
names.add("Doug");
names.add("Mike");
names.add("Janet");
names.add("Matt");
```

You need to use the add() method for each value. Adding a value will append it to the end of the collection. So, in the case of the preceding code, "Doug" is the first element, and "Matt" is the last. With ArrayLists, you can't use object notation using braces to add multiple items at once.

Get Elements in ArrayLists

To get an element, you use the get() method and pass in the integer of the element id number:

```
System.out.println(names.get(1)); // Outputs "Mike"
```

The preceding code takes the value at location 1 and then displays it on the screen. There is one catch however:

```
String myName = names.get(0);
```

The preceding code generates an error. The reason is because the values that are used with the ArrayList names are typed as Object. Object is the most basic class in Java; it defines everything else in the language, so in a way, everything in Java is an Object. Because the string myName is typed as String, there is a mismatch.

To get around this, we need to parse or convert the value to a String so it will be accepted. For Strings, we do this by chaining the toString() method; for numbers, we use their class' parse method:

```
String myName = names.get(0).toString();
System.out.println(myName);
```

This code takes the first value, element zero, and converts it to a String and then assigns it to the myName variable. The next line displays the value, "Doug".

Finally, unlike with arrays, you can display the contents of an `ArrayList` directly to the screen:

```
System.out.println(names);
```

This code will take all the values and display them on the screen like this:

```
[Doug, Mike, Janet, Matt]
```

Remove Elements from ArrayLists

Removing an element requires the `remove()` method, passing in the element number you want to remove:

```
names.remove(2);
```

In this case, the third (element number 2) value is removed from the `ArrayList`.

Find Items in ArrayLists

Unique to `ArrayLists`, you can search for items inside of it. It will go through the collection and return the element number of the first value that matches the search term you provide:

```
names.indexOf("Mike");
```

This will return an integer displaying the location of the value in the array.

Since these are all method calls, we can combine them together and nest their execution within other methods. So, if we wanted to find and remove an item based on the value, we can do that:

```
names.remove(names.indexOf("Mike"));
```

This code will first find the index number of "Mike" in the collection and then pass that value to the `remove()` method and take it out of the collection.

Replace Items in ArrayLists

You can use the set() method to replace items in an ArrayList by element index number:

```
names.set(1,"Sarah");
```

Again, you can combine methods together, so if you don't know the number of the element, you can use the indexOf() method:

```
names.set(names.indexOf("Matt"),"Sarah");
```

Get the Size of an ArrayList

The size() method returns the number of values in an ArrayList as an integer. It is the equivalent of the length property for an array:

```
names.size();
```

Copy Elements to a New ArrayList

The addAll() method will take all of the elements of one list and add them to a new list:

```
ArrayList newNames = new ArrayList();
newNames.addAll(names);
```

The new collection, newNames, starts off as an empty ArrayList, but after the addAll() method is called, it is now a copy of the names collection. The values aren't linked though. If a change is made to names, it isn't reflected in newNames. They are completely separate.

Clear an ArrayList

To remove all of the elements, not just values, you can use the clear() method:

```
names.clear();
```

After this code executes, the collection will be completely empty.

Code Examples

This code is also available on GitHub at the following location:

https://github.com/Apress/essential-java-AP-CompSci

Listing 48-1. Working with ArrayLists

```java
import java.util.ArrayList;

public class Main {

    public static void main(String[] args) {

        // Define an ArrayList
        ArrayList names = new ArrayList();

        // Add items
        names.add("Doug");
        names.add("Mike");
        names.add("Janet");
        names.add("Matt");

        // Get items
        System.out.println(names.get(1)); // Outputs "Mike"

        // Error due to type mismatch
        //String myName = names.get(0);

        // Working around the Object type with ArrayLists
        String myName = names.get(0).toString();
        System.out.println(myName);

        // Display all items
        System.out.println(names);

        // Remove item
        names.remove(2);
        System.out.println(names);

        // Find index of item by value
        System.out.println(names.indexOf("Mike"));
```

```java
        // Combine multiple methods together
        names.remove(names.indexOf("Mike"));
        System.out.println(names);

        // Replacing an item
        //names.set(1,"Sarah");
        names.set(names.indexOf("Matt"),"Sarah");
        System.out.println(names);

        // Get size, or number of items
        System.out.println(names.size());

        // Copy all values to new list
        ArrayList newNames = new ArrayList();
        newNames.addAll(names);
        System.out.println(names);
        System.out.println(newNames);

        // Clear all items
        names.clear();
        System.out.println(names.size());
    }
}

/* Output

Mike
Doug
[Doug, Mike, Janet, Matt]
[Doug, Mike, Matt]
1
[Doug, Matt]
[Doug, Sarah]
2
[Doug, Sarah]
[Doug, Sarah]
0

*/
```

Introducing Generics

The flexibility of ArrayLists over arrays makes it an attractive option for creating collections, but there are instances where the lack of type restrictions in a collection could be a problem. For instance, if you were working with a set of integer numbers, the fact that you can't prevent a string from entering the collection could make your code unintentionally complex and lead to bugs. In addition, because everything is typed as a generic Object class, you need to cast or parse everything in order to work with it:

```
ArrayList values = new ArrayList();

values.add(1);
values.add(2);
values.add("3"); // Perfectly legal, but undesired
values.add(4);

System.out.println(values);

int x = ((int) values.get(2)) / 2; // Because get(2) returns an Object
```

Instead, you can use the concept of generics, which can restrict an ArrayList instance to only contain certain types and provide a way for you to build strict typing to your collections and combine typing with the flexibility of the ArrayList.

Create an ArrayList with Generics

Generics are defined by identifying the type you want to work with and wrapping them in pointed brackets. Then you append these to the end of the ArrayList class definition when you create and initialize your ArrayList instance. Note that you need to use the full class name of the value type. You cannot use primitive types such as int, boolean, double, etc.:

```
ArrayList<Integer> numbers = new ArrayList<Integer>();
```

235

© Doug Winnie 2021
D. Winnie, *Essential Java for AP CompSci*, https://doi.org/10.1007/978-1-4842-6183-5_49

Now, when you add a type into the `ArrayList` using the `add()` method, you are restricted on the type you can put in:

```
numbers.add(1);
numbers.add(2);
numbers.add("3"); // Generates an error
numbers.add(4);
```

You still need to cast or parse values however, because the methods of the class still return `Object` types:

```
int y = ((int) values.get(2)) / 2;
```

But, you are now at least confident that the values that are stored in the collection are restricted to a specific type.

Typing Using Generics

Typing using generics defined the base type of the object. So, just like you would do with an array, or any other type, you can use generics to type collections that are part of a method definition by setting the parameters or return type using an ArrayList with generics.

The following method, for example, accepts an integer array as a parameter, but is typed to return an `ArrayList` typed as `Integer`:

```
public static ArrayList<Integer> convert(int[] data) {
    ArrayList<Integer> list = new ArrayList<Integer>();

    for (int i = 0; i < data.length; i++) {
        list.add(data[i]);
    }

    System.out.println(list);

    return list;
}
```

Code Examples

This code is also available on GitHub at the following location:

https://github.com/Apress/essential-java-AP-CompSci

Listing 49-1. Using ArrayLists with generics

```
import java.util.ArrayList;

public class Main {

    public static void main(String[] args) {

        ArrayList values = new ArrayList();

        values.add(1);
        values.add(2);
        //values.add("3"); // Perfectly legal, but undesired
        values.add(4);

        System.out.println(values);

        int x = ((int) values.get(2)) / 2; // Cast required since Object is
                                        returned

        ArrayList<Integer> numbers = new ArrayList<Integer>();
        numbers.add(1);
        numbers.add(2);
        //numbers.add("3"); // Generates an error
        numbers.add(4);

        int y = ((int) values.get(2)) / 2;

        // Create a new array
        int[] set = new int[] {1,2,3,4,5};
        // Convert that array to an ArrayList<Integer>
        ArrayList<Integer> newSet = convert(set);
    }
```

```java
public static ArrayList<Integer> convert(int[] data) {
    ArrayList<Integer> list = new ArrayList<Integer>();

    for (int i = 0; i < data.length; i++) {
        list.add(data[i]);
    }

    System.out.println(list);

    return list;
}
}
```

Looping with ArrayLists

Using a for loop with an ArrayList is pretty straightforward, but you need to work with two particular methods of the ArrayList class in order to loop through all of the elements.

Working with size() and get() Methods

ArrayLists, unlike arrays, use methods of the class instead of properties and bracket notation. When we work with an array, to get the size, we use the length property of the array. For ArrayList objects, we use the size() method, which returns an integer containing the number of items that are in the collection:

```
ArrayList<Integer> values = new ArrayList<Integer>();

values.add(5);
values.add(20);
values.add(75);
values.add(32);

System.out.println(values.size()); // 4
```

We can use the size() method to create the condition that controls how we loop through the collection.

With arrays, we have used bracket notation to access elements within the set; however, we don't have that option with the ArrayList. Instead, we need to work with the get() method and provide an integer to get a specific item from the set at that index number. With both of these methods, we can create our for loop to go through the items stored in the values collection from before:

```
for (int i = 0; i < values.size(); i++) {
    System.out.printf("Value: %d\n",values.get(i));
}
```

239

© Doug Winnie 2021
D. Winnie, *Essential Java for AP CompSci*, https://doi.org/10.1007/978-1-4842-6183-5_50

With both of these methods, we can now loop through the items using the for loop.

Code Examples

This code is also available on GitHub at the following location:

https://github.com/Apress/essential-java-AP-CompSci

Listing 50-1. Using ArrayList methods with a for loop

```java
import java.util.ArrayList;

public class Main {

    public static void main(String[] args) {

        ArrayList<Integer> values = new ArrayList<Integer>();

        values.add(5);
        values.add(20);
        values.add(75);
        values.add(32);

        System.out.println(values.size()); // 4

        for (int i = 0; i < values.size(); i++) {
            System.out.printf("Value: %d\n",values.get(i));
        }

    }
}

/* Output

4
Value: 5
Value: 20
Value: 75
Value: 32

*/
```

Using for...each Loops

When you have a collection, you have a group of stuff. When you sort through those items and need to go through them, ultimately, it doesn't matter how many there are, you still need to go through all of them.

You look at the pile of stuff, pick one up, do things with it, and then move on to the next item on the pile. Do you care which ordinal number it is? No. Do you care how many there are in total? Maybe, but you know that you just have to go through them all.

The for loop is a great type of loop for when you know precisely how many items you need to work with. Using the `size()` method of `ArrayLists` or the `length` property with arrays, you know how many you need to work with and can then numerically go through them all one by one.

But there is another way, and it is way simpler, and you don't need to keep track of so many things at once.

Mechanics of a for...each Loop

The `for...each` loop is similar in name, but different in structure. Think of it this way. You have a pile of shirts that you need to fold. That pile is called laundry. When you need to fold a shirt, you find a shirt, and it is in your hand. It doesn't matter which shirt in the laundry pile it is, but you know it's a shirt, and you call it foldMe.

You do your thing, folding your shirt the way you fold all of your shirts, and then put it away. You then go back to the laundry pile and get another shirt, this time a different shirt, but you still call it foldMe, because you are going through all of the shirts, and as you loop through all of them, you need to give it some sort of name.

A for...each loop is similar to a for loop, but different in terms of how it works through a collection of objects. Think of it like a pile of laundry. With a for loop, that pile of laundry needs to be arranged, so each shirt, sock, and pair of pants is in a specific order. You then go to each one, one by one, and perform an action, like folding them, and then go through them all.

© Doug Winnie 2021
D. Winnie, *Essential Java for AP CompSci*, https://doi.org/10.1007/978-1-4842-6183-5_51

But when it comes to laundry, it doesn't really matter what order you do them in. You just need to fold all the clothes. Arranging them into a specific order isn't particularly valuable. That is the difference of a for…each loop. In the preceding example, the for…each loop looks at the pile of laundry. It doesn't require that things be in a sequential order; it just picks up an item off the pile, and while it is in your hands, you can perform a specific task, like fold it, and then go back to the pile and grab another one. It does this until the pile is exhausted of items. In this case, it doesn't matter which one is first or last.

This Is the Mechanics of the for…each Loop

If we have a collection of `Strings`, we can loop through them using a `for...each` loop. Let's start with a new collection of names:

```
ArrayList<String> names = new ArrayList<String>();
names.add("Doug");
names.add("Mike");
```

This collection contains two names, both stored as `Strings`. We can then create our `for...each` loop to go through each item in the collection:

```
for (String name : names) {
    System.out.println(name);
}
```

When you look at this, read it this way: for each `String` in the collection names, perform these actions, referring to the current item as name.

Reading it this way, the section inside of the parentheses makes sense. You define the type of value you will be looping through in the collection. This is important so your program knows how to deal with different value types since integers, decimals, strings, and other types have different properties and methods. The colon is new and means that we are working with an item inside a collection. The colon defines which is the item and which is the collection. Item on the left, collection on the right.

Then, for the loop body, we refer to the item we are using from the collection by the name we defined at the top. In this case, by the identifier name.

We can then work with that object just like any other value of that value type, and if we change or update that value using the identifier, the change happens to the object in the collection, even after the loop is finished.

Often, you will work with data that has been formatted or analyzed before you use it in your program. One of the common ways to send and transmit information is using a delimited list.

In the preceding example, the program outputs each name on a different line.

ArrayLists Without Generics

One of the most flexible parts of `ArrayLists` is that they don't have to be typed. Each collection can contain a variety of different types. So, with a `for...each` loop, how do you go through them?

We have to remember that an untyped `ArrayList` is still typed, but it is typed with the most basic item in Java: the `Object` class. Using the `Object` class type, we can loop through all the items in the collection:

```
ArrayList values = new ArrayList();
values.add(5);
values.add(3.14159);
values.add('a');
values.add("Hello!");

for (Object item : values) {
    System.out.println(item);
}
```

In this example, the collection values have all kinds of different types, but because we create our `for...each` loop using the `Object` type, we can still work with each one, but only as `Object` instances.

Yep, Arrays Work Too

Using the `for...each` loop doesn't just stop with `ArrayList` collections, you can also use them with regular arrays. Just type the loop to the array type, and you can work with all the items using a more concise format:

```
int[] nums = new int[] {1,2,3,4,5,6};

for (int a : nums) {
    a *= a;
    System.out.println(a);
}
```

Again, the most flexible part of the for...each loop is that you don't need to worry about how many items are in the collection or set, and you don't need to work with each item by number, so if you are going through all of the items in a set, the for...each loop is a great option.

Code Examples

This code is also available on GitHub at the following location:

https://github.com/Apress/essential-java-AP-CompSci

Listing 51-1. Examples of the for...each loop

```
import java.util.ArrayList;

public class Main {

    public static void main(String[] args) {

        ArrayList<String> names = new ArrayList<String>();
        names.add("Doug");
        names.add("Mike");

        for (String name : names) {
            System.out.println(name);
        }

        ArrayList values = new ArrayList();
        values.add(5);
        values.add(3.14159);
        values.add('a');
        values.add("Hello!");
```

```java
        for (Object item : values) {
            System.out.println(item);
        }

        int[] nums = new int[] {1,2,3,4,5,6};

        for (int a : nums) {
            a *= a;
            System.out.println(a);
        }
    }
}

/* Output

Doug
Mike
5
3.14159
a
Hello!
1
4
9
16
25
36

*/
```

The Role-Playing Game Character

When we program multiple lines of code in a process, we refer to this as the program flow. As we run through our program, there is a flow, like the flow of a river that carries water from the origin to the river's end. A flow is how the program operates and what happens with values throughout our code.

But as we look at object-oriented programming, the approach is much different. We focus on the objects that we have in our program and how they work together to make our program work. The flow is still there, but it is encapsulated within each of the objects we work with. Each object has abilities that we can use with other objects.

But instead of getting bogged down in the specifics of object-oriented programming and become mired in jargon and terminology, let's build a model for how we can think about objects. A great example is building a role-playing game character.

What Is a Role-Playing Game Character?

When you play a role-playing game like *Dungeons & Dragons* or a computer game like *Warcraft* or *Elder Scrolls*, you create a "PC" or player character that will define your abilities and capabilities throughout the game. Typically, a role-playing character has several attributes or skills that have points associated with them. These points define how much of a skill that character has. When you play with one of these characters, you need to have enough points for various attributes or skills to perform certain actions. The chances of success for spells and actions are calculated based on the amount of skill points you have in your various attributes.

Player characters also are aligned under a player type, like a mage or a fighter. These types, or classes, define the initial strength and weakness of the skills for a character right from the beginning and define the type of actions that the player can do.

247

© Doug Winnie 2021
D. Winnie, *Essential Java for AP CompSci*, https://doi.org/10.1007/978-1-4842-6183-5_52

Let's start with something simple. Let's start with a simple mage.

A mage is a character that can cast magical spells across a wide range. A mage has a number of abilities that are unique from other classes like fighters. Let's say that a mage can have the following attributes:

- A mage has intelligence, required to be able to perform certain actions.

- A mage has strength; this determines how much the character can carry and how long they can survive in a fight.

- A mage has agility, which is used to calculate how quick they are able to move and potentially avoid attacks from enemies.

- A mage has wisdom, which is required to cast magical spells.

When you create a role-playing game character, you typically have a character sheet. This is where you keep track of all the stats for your player, the skills you have, the inventory of items you own, and other information. An example character sheet for a mage is at the end of this sprint section.

For the mage, we know we have five pieces of information we can keep track of. The first is the name of our mage. Then we will need to hold values for the intelligence, strength, agility, and wisdom skills.

With that, we have a basic framework for our character, or in this case a mage.

What we are building is a blueprint for not just a single mage, but for any mage that someone wants to play in the role-playing game. As we continue to build out this blueprint, we can add more information that would be part of every mage that is created through this template.

Filling Out Our Character Sheet with Data

With the basic Mage blueprint, we only know we want to store these attributes and skills, but we haven't said how we want to store them.

Just like with everything we do in programming, we need to explicitly define the type of value that is stored in each variable or object. For a role-playing game, we typically use integers or whole numbers to represent the various values in our player character.

There are also rules that define what the initial values of these attributes and skills are at the beginning of the game. Often these start with some sort of threshold, and then a form of random chance, like a die, is used to add to that threshold. This is called "rolling a character" in role-playing game jargon.

We can create a rule for how each of these is calculated. For every Mage character that is created, the rules are immediately put into action to help build the skills of the character.

Let's define the rules like this:

- Strength is 7, plus the value of a six-sided die is added.

- Intelligence is 15, plus the value of a six-sided die is added.

- Agility is 8, plus the value of a six-sided die is added.

- Wisdom is 10, plus the value of a six-sided die is added.

With these rules, we now have everything we need to calculate the skill stats for our player. To finish out our character, we need to add two more things. In most role-playing games, characters have two expendable assets. The first are called hit points or health. These show how healthy or how injured a player is. There is typically a maximum number that is calculated based on skills or abilities of the character, and then the current points, which creates a ratio showing the relative health of the player.

The second expendable asset is mana, or magic points. Mana is consumed when casting spells. The more advanced the spell is, the more mana points are consumed. Like with hit points, there is a maximum mana and current mana value, represented as a ratio to show the relative magical strength of a character. The maximum mana value is calculated based on the player's abilities.

For the mage, let's establish the hit point ceiling to be equal to the strength of the character.

Let's also set the mana ceiling to be equal to the intelligence and two times the wisdom of the character.

Now that these are finished, the character is ready to use. Following these rules was required for getting our character set up and all of the attributes and assets defined.

Classes, Instantiation, and Construction

With our mage character sheet, we have the rules and framework for what defines a mage character. Whenever we create a new mage, we can use this sheet to help create a new one.

You could create a large stack of empty sheets and create additional mages by taking a sheet off the top and completing the steps required to create the mage.

This process is a key part of object-oriented design. When we define the attributes, rules, and assets of the mage, we define the blueprint for every mage that can be created. This, in programming, is referred to as the class, or class design. In Java, we define what every mage would contain and the rules that apply, inside of a unique file that defines the class.

Every time we take a sheet off the stack and go through the rules to set up the player, we are instantiating the class. We are creating a unique instance of the class, based on the blueprint defined in the class, and customize it for that specific instance.

The steps we take when we create the class, from defining the initial attribute values by rolling a die to calculating the hit points and mana based on these attributes, are part of the construction of the class instance. These must happen before the class is able to be used, and this process is managed by the constructor, a special set of rules that kick off when you create a new instance of a class.

So, each character we make is a unique instance of a class, built using a set of rules contained in the constructor. This arrangement is the core part of object-oriented programming.

Player Character Sheets

Each of these character sheets represents one of the following classes:

- Mage
- Paladin
- Fighter
- Priest

Fighter

Name			Tank
Strength *(STR)*	Intelligence *(INT)*	Agility *(AGI)*	Constitution *(CON)*
15 + 6D	7 + 6D	8 + 6D	10 + 6D

Hit Points		Mana	
Current		Current	
Maximum		Maximum	
2(STR) + 2(CON)		0	

Mage

Name			Range
Strength *(STR)*	Intelligence *(INT)*	Agility *(AGI)*	Wisdom *(WIS)*
7 + 6D	15 + 6D	8 + 6D	10 + 6D

Hit Points		Mana	
Current		Current	
Maximum		Maximum	
(STR)		(INT) + 2(WIS)	

Paladin

	Tank
Name	
	Healer

Strength *(STR)*	Intelligence *(INT)*	Agility *(AGI)*	Wisdom *(WIS)*	Constitution *(CON)*
10 + 6D	15 + 6D	5 + 6D	10 + 6D	10 + 6D

Hit Points	Mana
Current	Current
Maximum	Maximum
(STR) + 2(CON)	(INT) + 2(WIS)

Priest

Name	Healer

Strength *(STR)*	Intelligence *(INT)*	Agility *(AGI)*	Charisma *(CHA)*
7 + 6D	15 + 6D	8 + 6D	10 + 6D

Hit Points	Mana
Current	Current
Maximum	Maximum
(STR)	(INT) + 2(CHA)

Polymorphism

When we work as individuals, we can only do so much. When we work together as a party, we can accomplish much more and use the unique talents that every member of the party has. While this is true in many life situations, it is especially true with role-playing games, and when you understand how to build a party using unique roles, you are applying object-oriented programming principles without even realizing it.

Creating a Class Hierarchy

In the previous sprint, we explored how a player character, or PC, is defined by a class. That class defines the blueprint for every instance of that class that can be created. But if we look at multiple classes side by side, we start to see some common things between them.

For instance, if we look at all of these, we can pull out all of the common elements. These include the name; the attributes for strength, intelligence, and agility; and the maximum and current hit points and mana. It is important to call out though that the presence of these across all of the classes is what is consistent. The rules that define the minimum values and the ways they are calculated are not the same—only the fact that they all exist.

But although these are all consistent in each player class, if we ever change the rules of our role-playing game and, say, add another common component, like experience or character level, we would need to add it to each player class and update each sheet.

Instead, we could take all of the common items and create a player sheet that contains just them, but doesn't include the rules for constructing the player character instance. Then, for each unique class, we can extend or build on the basic blueprint and add the unique rules that govern each one, as well as the unique attributes that are part of those specific classes.

© Doug Winnie 2021
D. Winnie, *Essential Java for AP CompSci*, https://doi.org/10.1007/978-1-4842-6183-5_53

This is called a class hierarchy. We have a generic player character class, and then add or extend that class, adding all of the unique elements that are part of the class we build on top. You can visualize this by creating a sheet with the common items that are part of the generic player class. Then using clear transparencies, add in the unique items on top of the paper, building out the class.

The paper underneath is called the superclass. It has a higher hierarchy. The transparency that extends the superclass is called the subclass. You can show them like an org chart, showing which subclasses extend from a superclass.

If we look at our five players, we have a collection of items, or objects. But what is common for all of the items in our collection? They all are instances of subclasses of a common superclass: the generic player class. So, you can say that all items in this collection must be instances of a subclass of the generic player character class.

But we have a problem. We now have a player character sheet that we can't use as a character instance. We can't take the generic player character and use it. It doesn't have any rules that define how it is created, so it is useless. In this case, we want the class only to be used a superclass to extend from, but we don't want to create instances of that class. To do that, we would call this class an abstract class. Abstract classes can't be instantiated, since they would be useless.

Party Up—All the Same—but All Different at the Same Time

With five instances of four different classes, we can start to play our role-playing game. But this game requires that we form a three-person party that are the active players in the game. Players can be substituted for one of the three players in the party, but only the players in the party are active in the game.

The rules for a party state that we need to have one tank, or a character that is designed to take extensive damage and use short-range melee style attacks; one range, or a character that attacks over a long range; and one healer, or a character that has a weak attack, but can heal other players in the party.

So, in order for us to put our player instances in the right position, we need a way to characterize them. These categories indicate that an instance from a class contains specific actions or values that are the same, making the class an implementer of the category, and that it contains all of the actions that are part of that category.

The category is called the interface, and it defines a unique set of requirements for a class to conform to the interface and that an instance can be used in a situation that requires a specific interface.

A class can implement one or many interfaces, like the paladin class. That implements two: tank and healer. So any player that is an instance of a paladin can be placed in either the tank or healer slot in the three-person party.

But we should call out something important here. For the healer or tank slots in the party, they are requiring the category or interface, not a specific class type. So more than one class can be put into that slot—it just needs to implement the interface that is required. This is called polymorphism, where we are using an interface as a way to support completely different classes, and we are restricting the slot to an interface, not to a specific class.

The Essential Tool: The Die

There is one last thing that we have used but haven't really called out. The die used to help construct our characters. The die was required to determine the values of each of the attributes of our player character instances.

But we didn't need to create an instance of a die; we just need to use it. We just want to take the die and roll it. We would call this action, of rolling the die, as a static action. We don't need to create a unique instance of the die in order to roll it. We can simply just roll it.

Class Hierarchy, Polymorphism, Abstract, and Static

Building off our basic object-oriented programming concepts of classes, instantiation, and construction, we can add more structure and flexibility. We can define classes, even classes that we can't create instances of, to serve as a superclass that other subclasses can extend and inherit the blueprint of the original class. We can also categorize classes using interfaces and use polymorphism to restrict objects based on interfaces instead of classes. Finally, we can create classes that have static actions that can be called without the need to create an instance of a class.

Next, we will put away the paper and pencil and dive into exactly how we would implement this in Java, rebuilding our role-playing game example, but this time in code.

Make All the Things… Classes

Now that we have a basic character class and our character sheets, we can start to learn how these can be created in Java as object-oriented classes.

Classes in Java define four main things:

1. What is the name of the class and how does it fit within the hierarchy and how is it classified using an interface

2. What are the values that are stored and used within each unique instance of the class

3. What are the actions that each unique instance of the class can perform

4. What rules govern how each unique instance is created during construction

Creating Some Class

We can start with the first, naming the class. In Java, we do that using the term `class` statement. Each unique class is typically stored as a specific file, generally with the same name as the class.

If we look at our mage character sheet, this gives us a good reference to use as we create the class.

In our IDE, we will need to create our project and then create a file for the class. This file would be called Mage.java.

© Doug Winnie 2021
D. Winnie, *Essential Java for AP CompSci*, https://doi.org/10.1007/978-1-4842-6183-5_54

When we create the file, we then need to populate the class name and then use the `class` statement. A code block, using braces, then surrounds the code that defines the blueprint for our class:

```
public class Mage {
}
```

We start with the `public` clause, since we want the class to be available within the program to use and create instances—we will cover more about the `public` clause in a bit. Then we follow with the `class` clause, and then the name of the class. Classes are usually capitalized, and each word is capitalized with no spaces. This is generally referred to as Pascal case.

Now that we have defined the basics of the class, we can start adding properties, or fields as they are sometimes called, to the class. These are essentially variables that will be unique for each instance of the class. Just like any other variable in Java, we need to type them to a primitive or class type and then give them a valid variable name.

We define these at the top of our class, within the class code block. If we look at our character sheet, we have nine items we need to add to our Mage class. These include the name of the character, the skill attributes, and the expendable assets for health and magic, remembering that health and magic each are two individual values, the maximum possible value and the current value for the instance.

To define these, we need to declare their access level, which in this case would be `public`. If you have worked previously with basic Java apps without classes, you might have had to use `public static`. For this class, we only need to use `public`:

```
public class Mage {
    // Name
    public String name;

    // Skill attributes
    public int strength;
    public int intelligence;
    public int agility;
    public int wisdom;

    // Health and magic
    public int maxHitPoints;
    public int hitPoints;
```

```
    public int maxMana;
    public int mana;
}
```

Now, for each instance of our class, we will have nine unique fields that we can use and store values. These are unique and exclusive to each instance, but each instance will have all nine of these fields.

Now, we need to tell our class how to build each instance or construct each instance. We do that with a special method called the constructor. The constructor method is the same name as the class and has a code block to contain all of the rules for how we construct each instance, just like a regular method.

The constructor is usually placed after the fields have been defined at the top of the class:

```
public class Mage {
    // Name
    public String name;

    // Skill attributes
    public int strength;
    public int intelligence;
    public int agility;
    public int wisdom;

    // Health and magic
    public int maxHitPoints;
    public int hitPoints;
    public int maxMana;
    public int mana;

    Mage() {
        // Constructor
    }
}
```

Inside the constructor, we can then create the specific rules for how we create each class instance. For example, the skill attributes are calculated based on a specific number and the value of a six-sided die. The hit points and mana are calculated based on the values of the skill attributes. If code in your class or constructor needs to work with classes outside of a basic program, you can include them in the project using the import statement at the top, just like with any other program. This program doesn't require it, but it is managed the same as we have seen before:

```java
public class Mage {
    // Name
    public String name;

    // Skill attributes
    public int strength;
    public int intelligence;
    public int agility;
    public int wisdom;

    // Health and magic
    public int maxHitPoints;
    public int hitPoints;
    public int maxMana;
    public int mana;

    Mage() {
        // Constructor
        strength = 7;
        intelligence = 15;
        agility = 8;

        wisdom = 10;

        strength += (int) (Math.random() * 6 + 1);
        intelligence += (int) (Math.random() * 6 + 1);
        agility += (int) (Math.random() * 6 + 1);
        wisdom += (int) (Math.random() * 6 + 1);

        maxHitPoints = hitPoints = strength;
        maxMana = mana = intelligence + (wisdom * 2);
    }
}
```

The last item we need to populate is the name. The name is something that we need to get more information on in order to create it. To do that, we can require that each time you create a mage, you need to provide a name, then that name is saved in the name field for the class instance. We can pass in a value into the constructor just like any Java method:

```java
public class Mage {
    // Name
    public String name;

    // Skill attributes
    public int strength;
    public int intelligence;
    public int agility;
    public int wisdom;

    // Health and magic
    public int maxHitPoints;
    public int hitPoints;
    public int maxMana;
    public int mana;

    Mage(String newName) {
        // Constructor
        name = newName;

        strength = 7;
        intelligence = 15;
        agility = 8;

        wisdom = 10;

        strength += (int) (Math.random() * 6 + 1);
        intelligence += (int) (Math.random() * 6 + 1);
        agility += (int) (Math.random() * 6 + 1);
        wisdom += (int) (Math.random() * 6 + 1);
```

```
        maxHitPoints = hitPoints = strength;
        maxMana = mana = intelligence + (wisdom * 2);
    }
}
```

Finally, we need our mage to be able to do something. We can create a method that will display the stats of our mage, so we can see the attributes and health information for our instance. We would create that as a regular method, providing a return type (which in this case is void), and then wrap everything in a code block. We can then refer to the values, or fields, in our class by their variable names:

```
public class Mage {
    // Name
    public String name;

    // Skill attributes
    public int strength;
    public int intelligence;
    public int agility;
    public int wisdom;

    // Health and magic
    public int maxHitPoints;
    public int hitPoints;
    public int maxMana;
    public int mana;

    Mage(String newName) {
        // Constructor
        name = newName;

        strength = 7;
        intelligence = 15;
        agility = 8;

        wisdom = 10;
```

```
    strength += (int) (Math.random() * 6 + 1);
    intelligence += (int) (Math.random() * 6 + 1);
    agility += (int) (Math.random() * 6 + 1);
    wisdom += (int) (Math.random() * 6 + 1);

    maxHitPoints = hitPoints = strength;
    maxMana = mana = intelligence + (wisdom * 2);
  }

  public void showStats() {
      System.out.println("---------------------------------");
      System.out.println(name + ", a mage:");
      System.out.println("      Strength: " + strength);
      System.out.println("Intelligence: " + intelligence);
      System.out.println("       Agility: " + agility);
      System.out.println("        Wisdom: " + wisdom);
      System.out.println("  Hit Points: " + hitPoints + " / " +
      maxHitPoints);
      System.out.println("          Mana: " + mana + " / " + maxMana);
      System.out.println();
  }
}
```

We now have a complete class. We have defined the class name, identified the fields in the class, specified the rules that govern how each class instance is created, and have given the class an action to perform.

Instantiate Thyself, Class!

To create an instance of our class, we need to then go back to where our main() method is in our program. In the past, we have always used the main() method to start our program, and generally in Java, the main() method is the consistent starting point for every program.

In another class file, in this case, I called mine Main.java, I have a standard main() method that will start the program. You'll notice this is not capitalized like the class name. This is unique to the main() method:

```
public class Main {
    public static void main(String[] args) {
    }
}
```

In my method, I can then create an instance of our new Mage class. Just like with any variable or container, I would need to define the type of value that is going to be stored in the variable. In this case, we would type it to the class. So the type is Mage. We then need to provide a name for the class instance, which I will call myMage. We then say that we are creating a new instance of the Mage class with the new clause and then trigger construction by calling the constructor method. Our constructor requires a String to be passed in with the character's name:

```
public class Main {
    public static void main(String[] args) {
        Mage myMage = new Mage("Francisco");
    }
}
```

We now have our first instance of the Mage class created! But if we run the program, nothing happens. To prove that we have an instance created, we can add a line to the constructor that outputs text to the screen when an instance is built. We can add this line to the end of our constructor:

```
public class Mage {
    // Name
    public String name;

    // Skill attributes
    public int strength;
    public int intelligence;
    public int agility;
    public int wisdom;

    // Health and magic
    public int maxHitPoints;
    public int hitPoints;
    public int maxMana;
    public int mana;
```

```
    Mage(String newName) {
        // Constructor
        name = newName;

        strength = 7;
        intelligence = 15;
        agility = 8;

        wisdom = 10;

        strength += (int) (Math.random() * 6 + 1);
        intelligence += (int) (Math.random() * 6 + 1);
        agility += (int) (Math.random() * 6 + 1);
        wisdom += (int) (Math.random() * 6 + 1);

        maxHitPoints = hitPoints = strength;
        maxMana = mana = intelligence + (wisdom * 2);

        System.out.println("A new mage named " + name + " has been created!");
    }

    public void showStats() {
        System.out.println("----------------------------------");
        System.out.println(name + ", a mage:");
        System.out.println("    Strength: " + strength);
        System.out.println("Intelligence: " + intelligence);
        System.out.println("     Agility: " + agility);
        System.out.println("      Wisdom: " + wisdom);
        System.out.println("  Hit Points: " + hitPoints + " / " +
        maxHitPoints);
        System.out.println("        Mana: " + mana + " / " + maxMana);
        System.out.println();
    }
}
```

Now if we run our program, we get this message in the output panel:

```
A new mage named Francisco has been created!

Process finished with exit code 0
```

We can then access and work with various fields in our program and execute actions that the instance can perform:

```java
public class Main {
    public static void main(String[] args) {
        Mage myMage = new Mage("Francisco");

        System.out.println(myMage.agility);

        myMage.showStats();
    }
}
```

We use the name of the class instance, myMage, to refer to the unique instance of the Mage class and then access the fields and methods of that instance to run our program.

```
A new mage named Francisco has been created!
14
-----------------------------------
Francisco, a mage:
    Strength: 10
Intelligence: 19
    Agility: 14
     Wisdom: 15
 Hit Points: 10 / 10
       Mana: 49 / 49

Process finished with exit code 0
```

Since we have a class, we can then create multiple instances of that class, referring to each one using a unique name:

```java
public class Main {
    public static void main(String[] args) {
        Mage myMage = new Mage("Francisco");
        myMage.showStats();
    }
}
```

```
        Mage myOtherMage = new Mage("Jaana");
        myOtherMage.showStats();
    }
}
```

Our two instances share identical blueprints, fields, methods, and constructors, but the values stored within it are unique and exclusive to that instance. So, when we run this program, we see the different values in each instance displayed on the screen:

```
A new mage named Francisco has been created!
----------------------------------
Francisco, a mage:
    Strength: 12
Intelligence: 19
    Agility: 13
     Wisdom: 16
 Hit Points: 12 / 12
       Mana: 51 / 51

A new mage named Jaana has been created!
----------------------------------
Jaanas, a mage:
    Strength: 13
Intelligence: 18
    Agility: 10
     Wisdom: 16
 Hit Points: 13 / 13
       Mana: 50 / 50

Process finished with exit code 0
```

With this basic class structure, we can then expand and build on it. For our game, we have four unique player character types. We have a mage, fighter, priest, and paladin. Each of these would be a unique class, and we can create a unique class file and definition for each one and then create as many instances of them as we want.

SPRINT 55

Class, Extend Thyself!

With our basic class created for the mage, we can look at other characters in our game and see how they compare to each other. We can see from their character sheets that they each have different skills and rules that govern how these skills are populated with values at the time of instantiation and construction.

The Mage class defines strength, intelligence, agility, and wisdom as the main fields and then uses a set of calculations to create their values and determine hit points and mana:

```java
public class Mage {
    // Name
    public String name;

    // Skill attributes
    public int strength;
    public int intelligence;
    public int agility;
    public int wisdom;

    // Health and magic
    public int maxHitPoints;
    public int hitPoints;
    public int maxMana;
    public int mana;

    Mage(String newName) {
        // Constructor
        name = newName;

        strength = 7;
        intelligence = 15;
        agility = 8;
```

© Doug Winnie 2021
D. Winnie, *Essential Java for AP CompSci*, https://doi.org/10.1007/978-1-4842-6183-5_55

```
        wisdom = 10;

        strength += (int) (Math.random() * 6 + 1);
        intelligence += (int) (Math.random() * 6 + 1);
        agility += (int) (Math.random() * 6 + 1);
        wisdom += (int) (Math.random() * 6 + 1);

        maxHitPoints = hitPoints = strength;
        maxMana = mana = intelligence + (wisdom * 2);

        System.out.println("A new mage named " + name + " has been created!");
    }

    public void showStats() {
        System.out.println("---------------------------------");
        System.out.println(name + ", a mage:");
        System.out.println("    Strength: " + strength);
        System.out.println("Intelligence: " + intelligence);
        System.out.println("     Agility: " + agility);
        System.out.println("      Wisdom: " + wisdom);
        System.out.println("  Hit Points: " + hitPoints + " / " + maxHitPoints);
        System.out.println("        Mana: " + mana + " / " + maxMana);
        System.out.println();
    }
}
```

Now, if we look at the `Fighter` class, we have a different set of skills that are used. The `Fighter` class defines strength, intelligence, agility, and constitution instead of wisdom. The calculations to determine their initial values and the amount of hit points and mana are also different:

```
public class Fighter {
    // Name
    public String name;

    // Skill attributes
    public int strength;
    public int intelligence;
```

```java
public int agility;
public int constitution;

// Health and magic
public int maxHitPoints;
public int hitPoints;
public int maxMana;
public int mana;

Fighter(String newName) {
    // Constructor
    name = newName;

    strength = 15;
    intelligence = 7;
    agility = 8;

    constitution = 10;

    strength += (int) (Math.random() * 6 + 1);
    intelligence += (int) (Math.random() * 6 + 1);
    agility += (int) (Math.random() * 6 + 1);
    constitution += (int) (Math.random() * 6 + 1);

    maxHitPoints = hitPoints = (strength * 2) + (constitution * 2);
    maxMana = mana = 0;

    System.out.println("A new fighter named " + name + " has been created!");
}

public void showStats() {
    System.out.println("----------------------------------");
    System.out.println(name + ", a fighter:");
    System.out.println("    Strength: " + strength);
    System.out.println("Intelligence: " + intelligence);
    System.out.println("     Agility: " + agility);
    System.out.println("Constitution: " + constitution);
    System.out.println("  Hit Points: " + hitPoints + " / " + maxHitPoints);
```

```
        System.out.println("              Mana: " + mana + " / " + maxMana);
        System.out.println();
    }
}
```

When you look at these two, there is a lot that is in common between them. They both contain a name, strength, intelligence, agility, hit points, and mana fields. They also both have a showStats() method that displays the instance's attribute values.

When you create classes, you can take things that are common for multiple classes and create superclasses. It works like this. If we create a class that has everything that is in common, we can then build what is unique for a Mage and a Fighter on top of what is common for both. When you create classes in this way, you can build on top of and include or extend the contents of these classes.

So, if we had a new class called PlayerCharacter, we can define that to include everything that is in common between Fighter and Mage:

```
public class PlayerCharacter {
    // Name
    public String name;

    // Skill attributes
    public int strength;
    public int intelligence;
    public int agility;

    // Health and magic
    public int maxHitPoints;
    public int hitPoints;
    public int maxMana;
    public int mana;

    PlayerCharacter() {
        System.out.println("A new player character has been created!");
    }

    public void showStats() {
    }
}
```

As you can see, only the things that are common across Mage and Fighter are included here. We define strength, intelligence, agility, hit points, and mana fields, and we have a constructor for the PlayerCharacter class, and we have a method for showStats() which doesn't do anything yet.

Now we can use this class as the foundation for other classes, including Mage and Fighter. We can strip out the items that are already in the PlayerCharacter class in each of these two classes. First, we can do that with the Mage class by removing the definitions for name, strength, intelligence, agility, hit points, and mana:

```java
public class Mage {
    // Skill attributes
    public int wisdom;

    Mage(String newName) {
        // Constructor
        name = newName;

        strength = 7;
        intelligence = 15;
        agility = 8;

        wisdom = 10;

        strength += (int) (Math.random() * 6 + 1);
        intelligence += (int) (Math.random() * 6 + 1);
        agility += (int) (Math.random() * 6 + 1);
        wisdom += (int) (Math.random() * 6 + 1);

        maxHitPoints = hitPoints = strength;
        maxMana = mana = intelligence + (wisdom * 2);

        System.out.println("A new mage named " + name + " has been created!");
    }

    public void showStats() {
        System.out.println("---------------------------------");
        System.out.println(name + ", a mage:");
        System.out.println("    Strength: " + strength);
        System.out.println("Intelligence: " + intelligence);
```

```
        System.out.println("      Agility: " + agility);
        System.out.println("       Wisdom: " + wisdom);
      System.out.println(" Hit Points: " + hitPoints + " / " + maxHitPoints);
        System.out.println("          Mana: " + mana + " / " + maxMana);
        System.out.println();
    }
}
```

When you do this though in an IDE, you will get errors appear, because Java doesn't know that you are building the Mage class on top of the PlayerCharacter class. Not yet at least:

```
Mage(String newName) {
    // Constructor
    name = newName;

    strength = 7;
    intelligence = 15;
    " Cannot resolve symbol 'intelligence'

    wisdom = 10;

    strength += (int) (Math.random() * 6 + 1);
    intelligence += (int) (Math.random() * 6 + 1);
    agility += (int) (Math.random() * 6 + 1);
    wisdom += (int) (Math.random() * 6 + 1);

    maxHitPoints = hitPoints = strength;
    maxMana = mana = intelligence + (wisdom * 2);

    System.out.println("A new mage named " + name + " has been created!");
}
```

We need to specifically define that we are building the Mage class on top of the PlayerCharacter class. We do that by changing the definition of the class on the first line.

When you build on top of another class, you are extending it, so we need to change the first line to read:

```
public class Mage extends PlayerCharacter {
```

When you do that, all the errors that we previously saw are resolved and go away, because everything that is part of the `PlayerCharacter` class is now included in the Mage class:

```
Mage(String newName) {
    // Constructor
    name = newName;

    strength = 7;
    intelligence = 15;
    agility = 8;

    wisdom = 10;

    strength += (int) (Math.random() * 6 + 1);
    intelligence += (int) (Math.random() * 6 + 1);
    agility += (int) (Math.random() * 6 + 1);
    wisdom += (int) (Math.random() * 6 + 1);

    maxHitPoints = hitPoints = strength;
    maxMana = mana = intelligence + (wisdom * 2);

    System.out.println("A new mage named " + name + " has been created!");
}
```

Let's go to our `Fighter` class now. Let's change the class definition at the top to include the `PlayerCharacter` class by changing the first line to read:

```
public class Fighter extends PlayerCharacter {
```

Now we can remove the items that are already in the `PlayerCharacter` class:

```
public class Fighter extends PlayerCharacter {
    // Skill attributes
    public int constitution;

    Fighter(String newName) {
        // Constructor
        name = newName;

        strength = 15;
        intelligence = 7;
        agility = 8;
```

```
        constitution = 10;

        strength += (int) (Math.random() * 6 + 1);
        intelligence += (int) (Math.random() * 6 + 1);
        agility += (int) (Math.random() * 6 + 1);
        constitution += (int) (Math.random() * 6 + 1);

        maxHitPoints = hitPoints = (strength * 2) + (constitution * 2);
        maxMana = mana = 0;

        System.out.println("A new fighter named " + name + " has been created!");
    }
    public void showStats() {
        System.out.println("---------------------------------");
        System.out.println(name + ", a fighter:");
        System.out.println("     Strength: " + strength);
        System.out.println("Intelligence: " + intelligence);
        System.out.println("      Agility: " + agility);
        System.out.println("Constitution: " + constitution);
        System.out.println("  Hit Points: " + hitPoints + " / " + maxHitPoints);
        System.out.println("         Mana: " + mana + " / " + maxMana);
        System.out.println();
    }
}
```

Everything looks good, so let's go to our `Main` class and update our `main()` method to create two instances of the `Mage` and `Fighter` class:

```
public class Main {
    public static void main(String[] args) {
        Mage myMage = new Mage("Francisco");
        myMage.showStats();

        Mage myOtherMage = new Mage("Jaana");
        myOtherMage.showStats();

        Fighter myFighter = new Fighter("Dupre");
        myFighter.showStats();
```

```
        Fighter myOtherFighter = new Fighter("Sentri");
        myOtherFighter.showStats();
    }
}
```

Now let's run and see what the output is. Remember that the values are generated using a random number, so these results will vary from others:

```
A new player character has been created!
A new mage named Francisco has been created!
---------------------------------
Francisco, a mage:
    Strength: 12
Intelligence: 17
    Agility: 9
     Wisdom: 16
 Hit Points: 12 / 12
       Mana: 49 / 49

A new player character has been created!
A new mage named Jaana has been created!
---------------------------------
Jaana, a mage:
    Strength: 12
Intelligence: 16
    Agility: 11
     Wisdom: 15
 Hit Points: 12 / 12
       Mana: 46 / 46

A new player character has been created!
A new fighter named Dupre has been created!
---------------------------------
Dupre, a fighter:
    Strength: 18
Intelligence: 9
```

```
      Agility: 12
 Constitution: 12
   Hit Points: 60 / 60
         Mana: 0 / 0
```

A new player character has been created!
A new fighter named Sentri has been created!

Sentri, a fighter:
```
     Strength: 18
 Intelligence: 12
      Agility: 13
 Constitution: 11
   Hit Points: 58 / 58
         Mana: 0 / 0
```

Process finished with exit code 0

You'll see that everything is looking good and everything is almost identical to what we did before, with one main difference. You'll see a new line "A new player character has been created!" at the top of each section when a new instance is constructed.

That line is located in our PlayerCharacter class constructor. When we create a class that is built on top of another class, it will run the contents of the base class constructor and then the code in the class it is built on top of.

But if we try to do that with the showStats() method, the same behavior doesn't happen. For example, change the PlayerCharacter showStats() method to add a new statement to the output console:

```
public class PlayerCharacter {
    // Name
    public String name;

    // Skill attributes
    public int strength;
    public int intelligence;
    public int agility;

    // Health and magic
```

```
    public int maxHitPoints;
    public int hitPoints;
    public int maxMana;
    public int mana;

    PlayerCharacter() {
        System.out.println("A new player character has been created!");
    }

    public void showStats() {
        System.out.println("Here are the stats for, " + name);
    }
}
```

If you run the program again, the code in the PlayerCharacter showStats() method is never displayed. When you build on top of a class and want to run code from a method it is built on top of, you need to specifically state you want to run it. A constructor will automatically run the code in the base class without you needing to do anything.

To call the code in a base class' matching method, you need to use the super statement. Let's update the Mage class to see how this works:

```
public class Mage extends PlayerCharacter {
    // Skill attributes
    public int wisdom;

    Mage(String newName) {
        // Constructor
        name = newName;

        strength = 7;
        intelligence = 15;
        agility = 8;

        wisdom = 10;

        strength += (int) (Math.random() * 6 + 1);
        intelligence += (int) (Math.random() * 6 + 1);
        agility += (int) (Math.random() * 6 + 1);
        wisdom += (int) (Math.random() * 6 + 1);
```

```
        maxHitPoints = hitPoints = strength;
        maxMana = mana = intelligence + (wisdom * 2);

        System.out.println("A new mage named " + name + " has been created!");
    }
    public void showStats() {
        super.showStats();
        System.out.println("----------------------------------");
        System.out.println(name + ", a mage:");
        System.out.println("    Strength: " + strength);
        System.out.println("Intelligence: " + intelligence);
        System.out.println("     Agility: " + agility);
        System.out.println("      Wisdom: " + wisdom);
        System.out.println("  Hit Points: " + hitPoints + " / " +
        maxHitPoints);
        System.out.println("        Mana: " + mana + " / " + maxMana);
        System.out.println();
    }
}
```

You'll see that the showStats() method has a call at the beginning:

```
super.showStats();
```

This will go to the class that this class extends and execute the method. If we run this program, we can see how this works:

```
A new player character has been created!
A new mage named Francisco has been created!
Here are the stats for, Francisco
----------------------------------
Francisco, a mage:
    Strength: 13
Intelligence: 19
     Agility: 12
      Wisdom: 16
  Hit Points: 13 / 13
        Mana: 51 / 51
```

A new player character has been created!
A new mage named Jaana has been created!
Here are the stats for, Jaana

Jaana, a mage:
     Strength: 9
 Intelligence: 18
      Agility: 12
       Wisdom: 15
   Hit Points: 9 / 9
         Mana: 48 / 48

A new player character has been created!
A new fighter named Dupre has been created!

Dupre, a fighter:
     Strength: 18
 Intelligence: 8
      Agility: 13
 Constitution: 16
   Hit Points: 68 / 68
         Mana: 0 / 0

A new player character has been created!
A new fighter named Sentri has been created!

Sentri, a fighter:
     Strength: 18
 Intelligence: 9
      Agility: 9
 Constitution: 13
   Hit Points: 62 / 62
         Mana: 0 / 0

Process finished with exit code 0

If you notice, only the mages that are created display the "Here are the stats for…" line. That is because we haven't added the `super.showStats()` call to the `Fighter` class, only to the `Mage` class.

When you create classes like this that extend other classes, you are creating a class hierarchy. The base class is called the superclass. The class that you create that extends the superclass is called the subclass.

So, in our example, `PlayerCharacter` is the superclass. `Mage` and `Fighter` are subclasses of the `PlayerCharacter` superclass.

When we use the `super` statement, we are asking the superclass to do something, in this case, the `PlayerCharacter` class.

You can create as many subclasses of a superclass as you want, and you can continue to extend classes as far as you need to.

SPRINT 56

I Don't Collect Those; Too Abstract

When you play a role-playing game, you work together as a team with other people. This could be with other players in the same room in real life or simulated characters in a computer game. A party is a collection, a group of people who have something in common.

In Java, we can create collections using arrays or ArrayLists. These collections can be of everything, and we can use them to create collections of things that we define ourselves using classes. Java collections aren't limited to things that are just in the core language—they can be instances of objects that we create in our own custom classes.

Here is an example, in our program, we can create a collection of characters in our game, called party:

```java
import java.util.ArrayList;

public class Main {

    public static ArrayList party;

    public static void main(String[] args) {
        party = new ArrayList();

        party.add(new Mage("Jaana"));
        party.add(new Mage("Antos"));
    }
}
```

In this example, we now have a collection called party, and it contains two instances of the Mage class. Party on! Well—not quite.

© Doug Winnie 2021
D. Winnie, *Essential Java for AP CompSci*, https://doi.org/10.1007/978-1-4842-6183-5_56

When we create an `ArrayList` without generics, we are typing the collection to `Object`, meaning that anything can be added to it, including a number, string, or any object in Java. It also means that we can't access the unique methods that are part of the Mage class, like `showStats()`. So if we try to add this line:

```
party.get(0).showStats();
```

we get an error, because it can't find that method in the class that defines the collection: the `Object` class.

But, we can fix this. Using generics, we can type the `ArrayList` collection to the Mage type, then we can access the methods of Mage. We can update our code to read like this:

```
import java.util.ArrayList;

public class Main {

    public static ArrayList<Mage> party;

    public static void main(String[] args) {
        party = new ArrayList<Mage>();

        party.add(new Mage("Jaana"));
        party.add(new Mage("Antos"));
    }
}
```

Now we can use the methods that are part of the Mage class, and we can even use a `for...each` loop to go through each of the objects in the collection:

```
import java.util.ArrayList;

public class Main {

    public static ArrayList<Mage> party;

    public static void main(String[] args) {
        party = new ArrayList<Mage>();

        party.add(new Mage("Jaana"));
        party.add(new Mage("Antos"));
```

```
    for (Mage pc : party)
        pc.showStats();
    }
}
```

When I run this, I can get the output for each of the two Mage class instances that are now in the collection:

```
A new player character has been created!
A new mage named Jaana has been created!
A new player character has been created!
A new mage named Antos has been created!
Here are the stats for, Jaana
----------------------------------
Jaana, a mage:
    Strength: 13
Intelligence: 21
     Agility: 10
      Wisdom: 14
  Hit Points: 13 / 13
        Mana: 49 / 49

Here are the stats for, Antos
----------------------------------
Antos, a mage:
    Strength: 9
Intelligence: 20
     Agility: 13
      Wisdom: 15
  Hit Points: 9 / 9
        Mana: 50 / 50

Process finished with exit code 0
```

But we still have a problem. What about other classes? If I want to create a Fighter and add them to the collection, I can't:

```
party.add(new Fighter("Sentri"));
```

The following code gives me an error, because the ArrayList collection is specifically typed to a Mage. So how do we fix this?

We need to think back to how we built the Mage and Fighter and other potential classes. We built them to extend the PlayerCharacter class, so, with that in mind, what are Mage and Fighter? They are PlayerCharacters! We can use the superclass as a tool to type any collection or object to accept any of the subclasses that extend it. We will also need to update our for...each loop, because it will need to look for PlayerCharacters in the collection, not a unique class like the Mage class:

```
import java.util.ArrayList;

public class Main {

    public static ArrayList<PlayerCharacter> party;

    public static void main(String[] args) {
        party = new ArrayList<PlayerCharacter>();

        party.add(new Mage("Jaana"));
        party.add(new Mage("Antos"));
        party.add(new Fighter("Sentri"));

        for (PlayerCharacter pc : party)
            pc.showStats();
    }
}
```

Now we can support multiple character types in our collection by typing it to the superclass. The collection can now hold the Mage and Fighter instances because they extend the PlayerCharacter superclass.

There is one important thing to note though. The showStats() method that we access in the for...each loop works, because it is located in the superclass. If we didn't have that method in PlayerCharacter, we wouldn't be able to use it, so if you know that you will have subclasses that have a method and will need to type collections and objects to a superclass, it is helpful to create empty methods so you can work with them.

But, we have one more issue. The collection can now support any class that extends PlayerCharacter—but that includes the PlayerCharacter class itself. We have designed PlayerCharacter to serve as a foundation to build our Mage, Fighter, and other classes from. We don't want to be able to create instances of PlayerCharacter:

```
import java.util.ArrayList;

public class Main {

    public static ArrayList<PlayerCharacter> party;

    public static void main(String[] args) {
        party = new ArrayList<PlayerCharacter>();

        party.add(new Mage("Jaana"));
        party.add(new Mage("Antos"));
        party.add(new Fighter("Sentri"));
        party.add(new PlayerCharacter());

        for (PlayerCharacter pc : party)
            pc.showStats();
    }
}
```

In this example, we can create an instance of PlayerCharacter, which we never intended, and as a result, we get some strange output at the end when we run our program:

```
A new player character has been created!
A new mage named Jaana has been created!
A new player character has been created!
A new mage named Antos has been created!
A new player character has been created!
A new fighter named Sentri has been created!
A new player character has been created!
Here are the stats for, Jaana
------------------------------------
Jaana, a mage:
    Strength: 12
Intelligence: 17
     Agility: 10
      Wisdom: 12
  Hit Points: 12 / 12
        Mana: 41 / 41
```

```
Here are the stats for, Antos
------------------------------------
Antos, a mage:
    Strength: 9
Intelligence: 16
     Agility: 13
      Wisdom: 12
  Hit Points: 9 / 9
        Mana: 40 / 40

------------------------------------
Sentri, a fighter:
    Strength: 18
Intelligence: 9
     Agility: 9
Constitution: 12
  Hit Points: 60 / 60
        Mana: 0 / 0

Here are the stats for, null

Process finished with exit code 0
```

We need to find a way to have the `PlayerCharacter` class, but prevent our program from allowing us to create instances of it. The answer is to make it an abstract class. The abstract clause is added to the first line of a class definition:

```
public abstract class PlayerCharacter {
    // Name
    public String name;

    // Skill attributes
    public int strength;
    public int intelligence;
    public int agility;
```

```
// Health and magic
public int maxHitPoints;
public int hitPoints;
public int maxMana;
public int mana;

PlayerCharacter() {
    System.out.println("A new player character has been created!");
}

public void showStats() {
    System.out.println("Here are the stats for, " + name);
}
}
```

With the class now defined as abstract, we can extend it to build subclasses, but we can't create instances of it on its own:

```
party.add(new PlayerCharacter());
```

So this line of code now generates an error, stating that it is abstract, and can't be instantiated. We still can type collections and other objects to it though—which is perfectly legal—because we aren't creating new instances of the PlayerCharacter class; we are simply allowing its subclasses to work with it.

Access Denied: Protected and Private

When we create classes, we are creating a blueprint for how each instance will operate and the data that it will contain. It also defines the rules for how a programmer can access that data and provide protections for the fields that are inside of it.

Before we dive into the code, let's refer back to our role-playing game example. When a player achieves certain activities like defeating enemies, completing quests, or attaining key items, they gain experience points, or XP. These points define what level your character is, and with each new level you attain, you can do more and more with your character in the game.

In addition, when a player increases in level, or "levels up," one of their skill attributes usually increases as well, like strength, agility, intelligence, or others. This then affects the health and magic values for the character since they are calculated based on the attributes. It is important to note, however, that the process of leveling up only happens when experience points have passed a certain threshold.

So, we are going to create the ability to add experience points, level up, boost attributes when leveling up, and recalculate health and magic points upon leveling up.

The rules for how this works vary across games, so for this example, we will keep it fairly simple. A player starts with zero experience points and at level one. With each 1000 experience points, the player increases in level. When a character levels up, one of the player class skill attributes will increase by one, for instance, strength. When the attribute increases, the maximum health and mana points are calculated and are replenished to full value.

This example is going to require more rework of our existing code, called refactoring. So follow along carefully as we go through this example.

© Doug Winnie 2021
D. Winnie, *Essential Java for AP CompSci*, https://doi.org/10.1007/978-1-4842-6183-5_57

The first thing we need to do is add the fields for experience points and level of the character. Since these are universal for all characters, we can place them in the PlayerCharacter class:

```
public abstract class PlayerCharacter {
    // Name
    public String name;

    // Skill attributes
    public int strength;
    public int intelligence;
    public int agility;

    // Health and magic
    public int maxHitPoints;
    public int hitPoints;
    public int maxMana;
    public int mana;

    // Experience
    public int xp;
    public int level;

    PlayerCharacter() {}

    public void showStats() {}
}
```

With these two values, we can now start holding our experience for characters.

But I want to take a step back and think about how we have created this class. In every single one of these fields, we have defined them as public. When a field, method, or member of a class is defined as public, that means that they are fully accessible through the class instance. So, there would be nothing to stop me from doing this:

```
Fighter pc = new Fighter("Dupre");
pc.level = 100;
```

We don't want that to be possible. In fact, we don't want any of our attributes to be publicly accessible to change in our program. The ability to do that should be within the class only.

The way to do this is to change the keyword `public` to `private`. This will render the class member to only be accessible within the class, and it blocks access from the outside. So, we can change our program to make these private:

```
// Experience
private int xp;
private int level;
```

The `private` statement now makes this work only within the class. So the previous example where we were able to access the level field publicly would generate an error.

There is one issue that exists, but isn't apparent yet. Let's add some code to show what the issue is.

The `Fighter` class extends `PlayerCharacter`, and the `showStats()` method displays the stats for the character on the screen:

```java
public class Fighter extends PlayerCharacter {
    // Skill attributes
    public int constitution;

    Fighter(String newName) {
        // Constructor
        name = newName;

        strength = 15;
        intelligence = 7;
        agility = 8;

        constitution = 10;

        strength += (int) (Math.random() * 6 + 1);
        intelligence += (int) (Math.random() * 6 + 1);
        agility += (int) (Math.random() * 6 + 1);
        constitution += (int) (Math.random() * 6 + 1);

        maxHitPoints = hitPoints = (strength * 2) + (constitution * 2);
        maxMana = mana = 0;

        System.out.println("A new fighter named " + name + " has been created!");
    }
```

```java
    public void showStats() {
        System.out.println("----------------------------------");
        System.out.printf("%s, a fighter:\n", name );
        System.out.printf("STR: %d | INT: %d | AGI: %d | CON: %d | HP: %d /
        %d | MP: %d / %d\n",
                strength, intelligence, agility, constitution, hitPoints,ma
                xHitPoints,mana,maxMana);
        System.out.println();
    }
}
```

We can update this to display the experience and level of the player:

```java
public void showStats() {
    System.out.println("-----------------------------------");
    System.out.printf("%s, a level %d fighter with %d XP:\n", name,
    level, xp );
    System.out.printf("STR: %d | INT: %d | AGI: %d | CON: %d | HP: %d / %d
    | MP: %d / %d\n",
            strength, intelligence, agility, constitution, hitPoints,maxHit
            Points,mana,maxMana);
    System.out.println();
}
```

If we add this code to display the level and xp fields, we get an error. The fact that they are private in the superclass, `PlayerCharacter`, doesn't give them access to any subclasses. They can only be accessed within instances of the `PlayerCharacter` class, which isn't possible, since we made it an abstract class.

Our way around this is to use the `protected` statement instead of `private`. Members that are made protected are available to the class where they are defined as well as subclasses that extend it. So we would need to go back and change it to `protected`, and we can do the same for all of the other attributes as well:

```java
public abstract class PlayerCharacter {
    // Name
    protected String name;
```

```
    // Skill attributes
    protected int strength;
    protected int intelligence;
    protected int agility;

    // Health and magic
    protected int maxHitPoints;
    protected int hitPoints;
    protected int maxMana;
    protected int mana;

    // Experience
    protected int xp;
    protected int level;

    PlayerCharacter() {}

    public void showStats() {}
}
```

Now all of the character attributes are protected, meaning that they can only be accessed within the class or within any subclasses that extend it.

We need to update our Fighter class to make the exclusive attributes there, in this case the constitution field, to private. Why private? Because this class isn't extended, so we can use private for the Fighter class:

```
// Skill attributes
private int constitution;
```

We can then add support for the xp and level attributes in our Fighter class constructor:

```
Fighter(String newName) {
    // Constructor
    name = newName;

    strength = 15;
    intelligence = 7;
    agility = 8;
```

```
    constitution = 10;

    strength += (int) (Math.random() * 6 + 1);
    intelligence += (int) (Math.random() * 6 + 1);
    agility += (int) (Math.random() * 6 + 1);
    constitution += (int) (Math.random() * 6 + 1);

    maxHitPoints = hitPoints = (strength * 2) + (constitution * 2);
    maxMana = mana = 0;

    xp = 0;
    level = 1;

    System.out.println("A new fighter named " + name + " has been created!");
}
```

With the fields now available, we can define our methods for increasing the experience points for our character instances. We can create a new method called addXP() for our Fighter class. We want to make this method public because we will need to access this using each instance of the class in our main program:

```
public void addXP(int deltaXP) {
    if (deltaXP < 0) {
        System.out.println("ERROR: Invalid experience delta value");
        return;
    }
    xp += deltaXP;
    level = (int) (xp / 1000) + 1;
}
```

We have created this so we can provide some protection for our program. The addXP() method accepts an integer value for the amount of experience points to add. We then have a conditional to ensure that the value is equal to or greater than zero. This is important because we are creating a safe way to manipulate the xp field value without providing full public access to it. We also are creating a way to control how the values of multiple fields can be affected using a single action. This is a common practice, where you provide a public method-based access to private or protected fields in a class instance.

In this case, we are increasing the xp value and setting the level based on the rules we defined earlier.

In this method, we also want a way to trigger the player to level up if they earned enough experience points. So we can add a new method to do that; we will call it levelUp(). But before we build it, we need to consider how it should be used. We want to make sure that the levelUp() method is private, because we don't want the ability to trigger this publicly. We only want the method to be available within the class instance. Methods can be defined as public, private, or protected, just like fields. So we could write the code like this:

```
public void addXP(int deltaXP) {
    if (deltaXP < 0) {
        System.out.println("ERROR: Invalid experience delta value");
        return;
    }
    xp += deltaXP;
    level = (int) (xp / 1000) + 1;

    if (xp % 1000 >= deltaXP)
        levelUp();
}

private void levelUp() {
    int attribute = (int) (Math.random() * 4);
    if (attribute == 0) strength++;
    if (attribute == 1) intelligence++;
    if (attribute == 2) agility++;
    if (attribute == 3) constitution++;
}
```

Now we have created the ability to level up our character. We first accept an increase in experience and then execute a private method called levelUp(). It selects a random attribute and increases its value by one.

The next thing we need to do is take the calculations for the health and magic points and run those again. Those are defined in the constructor, but we can pull them out and create a private method so we can access the rules in multiple places in the program:

```java
public class Fighter extends PlayerCharacter {
    // Skill attributes
    public int constitution;

    Fighter(String newName) {
        // Constructor
        name = newName;

        strength = 15;
        intelligence = 7;
        agility = 8;

        constitution = 10;

        strength += (int) (Math.random() * 6 + 1);
        intelligence += (int) (Math.random() * 6 + 1);
        agility += (int) (Math.random() * 6 + 1);
        constitution += (int) (Math.random() * 6 + 1);

        xp = 0;
        level = 1;

        calcHPMP();

        System.out.println("A new fighter named " + name + " has been
        created!");
    }

    public void showStats() {
        System.out.println("----------------------------------");
        System.out.printf("%s, a level %d fighter with %d XP:\n", name,
        level, xp );
        System.out.printf("STR: %d | INT: %d | AGI: %d | CON: %d | HP: %d /
        %d | MP: %d / %d\n",
                strength, intelligence, agility, constitution, hitPoints,
                maxHitPoints,mana,maxMana);
        System.out.println();
    }
```

```java
    public void addXP(int deltaXP) {
        int oldLevel = level;
        if (deltaXP < 0) {
            System.out.println("ERROR: Invalid experience delta value");
            return;
        }
        xp += deltaXP;
        level = (int) (xp / 1000) + 1;

        if (oldLevel != level)
            levelUp();
    }

    private void levelUp() {
        int attribute = (int) (Math.random() * 4);
        if (attribute == 0) strength++;
        if (attribute == 1) intelligence++;
        if (attribute == 2) agility++;
        if (attribute == 3) constitution++;
        calcHPMP();
    }

    private void calcHPMP() {
        maxHitPoints = hitPoints = (strength * 2) + (constitution * 2);
        maxMana = mana = 0;
    }
}
```

The last thing we need to consider is how we are building our collections, or our party. Since we are typing everything to the superclass, we need to make sure that methods that we are accessing in the subclass have stubs in the superclass. This would apply for the addXP() method.

Since the error checking and overall value adjustments are universal, we can move those to the superclass. The call to levelUp() we would need to keep in the subclass since we are calling a method that is private to the class, in this case the Fighter class.

So in the Fighter class, we would change it to

```
public void addXP(int deltaXP) {
    int oldLevel = level;
    super.addXP(deltaXP);

    if (oldLevel != level)
        levelUp();
}
```

And then in the PlayerCharacter class, we would add

```
protected void addXP(int deltaXP) {
    if (deltaXP < 0) {
        System.out.println("ERROR: Invalid experience delta value");
        return;
    }
    xp += deltaXP;
    level = (int) (xp / 1000) + 1;
}
```

With these all created, we can put them into action. We can create a party with a single character and run a loop, adding in a random amount of experience points, and see if everything works.

In our Main class, we can then build the party and run the loop:

```
import java.util.ArrayList;

public class Main {

    public static ArrayList<PlayerCharacter> party;

    public static void main(String[] args) {
        party = new ArrayList<PlayerCharacter>();

        party.add(new Fighter("Sentri"));

        for (PlayerCharacter pc : party)
            pc.showStats();
```

```
    int turns = 10;
    for (int i = 1; i <= turns; i++)
    {
        System.out.println("Turn #"+ i);
        for (PlayerCharacter pc : party)
        {
            pc.addXP((int) (Math.random() * 1000));
            pc.showStats();
        }
    }
}
```

Now our program will create a single person party, and then for ten turns, add a random number of experience points, and display the stats after each turn. If everything works, we should see the experience, level, attributes, and magic/health values to go up over time:

```
A new fighter named Sentri has been created!
---------------------------------
Sentri, a level 1 fighter with 0 XP:
STR: 19 | INT: 11 | AGI: 11 | CON: 13 | HP: 64 / 64 | MP: 0 / 0

Turn #1
---------------------------------
Sentri, a level 1 fighter with 523 XP:
STR: 19 | INT: 11 | AGI: 11 | CON: 13 | HP: 64 / 64 | MP: 0 / 0

Turn #2
---------------------------------
Sentri, a level 2 fighter with 1278 XP:
STR: 19 | INT: 11 | AGI: 12 | CON: 13 | HP: 64 / 64 | MP: 0 / 0

Turn #3
---------------------------------
Sentri, a level 3 fighter with 2068 XP:
STR: 19 | INT: 11 | AGI: 13 | CON: 13 | HP: 64 / 64 | MP: 0 / 0
```

Turn #4

Sentri, a level 3 fighter with 2957 XP:
STR: 19 | INT: 11 | AGI: 13 | CON: 13 | HP: 64 / 64 | MP: 0 / 0

Turn #5

Sentri, a level 4 fighter with 3124 XP:
STR: 19 | INT: 11 | AGI: 14 | CON: 13 | HP: 64 / 64 | MP: 0 / 0

Turn #6

Sentri, a level 4 fighter with 3413 XP:
STR: 19 | INT: 11 | AGI: 14 | CON: 13 | HP: 64 / 64 | MP: 0 / 0

Turn #7

Sentri, a level 5 fighter with 4210 XP:
STR: 19 | INT: 11 | AGI: 14 | CON: 14 | HP: 66 / 66 | MP: 0 / 0

Turn #8

Sentri, a level 5 fighter with 4402 XP:
STR: 19 | INT: 11 | AGI: 14 | CON: 14 | HP: 66 / 66 | MP: 0 / 0

Turn #9

Sentri, a level 6 fighter with 5393 XP:
STR: 20 | INT: 11 | AGI: 14 | CON: 14 | HP: 68 / 68 | MP: 0 / 0

Turn #10

Sentri, a level 6 fighter with 5414 XP:
STR: 20 | INT: 11 | AGI: 14 | CON: 14 | HP: 68 / 68 | MP: 0 / 0

Process finished with exit code 0

In this example, we can see that the level increased at turns 2, 3, 5, 7, and 9. The attributes then increased, with the hit points increasing as well when the constitution and strength attributes increased at turns 7 and 9.

Finally, as a test, we can confirm that our error handler works correctly too. If we add the following line to our program:

```
party.get(0).addXP(-100);
```

We will then get the following error code in our program output:

```
ERROR: Invalid experience delta value
```

While keeping everything public in your program might seem easiest, it can lead to unpredictable results and make your program harder to use and confusing to build. Using the `private` and `protected` statements, you can keep class members such as fields and methods from having external access and ensure that your programs work the way you designed them to.

Interfacing with Interfaces

When we originally defined our game, we created the concept of a party. In many role-playing games, the party is the group of active players who are working together to complete quests, defeat enemies, and progress through the game.

We defined the party as requiring three types of characters. The first is a tank, which is a character that can take a lot of damage but can only attack at short range. The second is a range, which is a character that cannot take a lot of damage but can attack from a distance. The last is a healer, which can heal the injuries sustained by another party member.

What is interesting about these types is that they can apply to more than one type of character class. Take the Paladin class, for example, that is a tank and a healer, so we need to have a way to create instances of character classes but have a way to categorize them so they can be interchanged with other classes in a typed container.

We have a basic ArrayList to hold our party, but let's create a new class to handle all of our Party characteristics:

```java
public class Party {

    Party() {}
}
```

Inside of this class, we will need to create variables for each type of character that forms the party. Let's start with one, the tank. We can create a class-scoped variable called tank and type it to the PlayerCharacter class:

```java
public class Party {

    PlayerCharacter tank;

    Party() {}
}
```

© Doug Winnie 2021

D. Winnie, *Essential Java for AP CompSci*, https://doi.org/10.1007/978-1-4842-6183-5_58

While this wouldn't create any syntax or runtime errors, it does go against the rules we created for the class. We only want two types of characters to be allowed as a tank: the paladin and fighter. So how do we create a way to type to just these?

The answer is to create an interface.

Interfaces are separate Java files that you apply or implement with a class. That then tells Java that this class applies all of the requirements defined by the interface, and you can then type containers, collections, or anything that you can type to an interface.

Creating an interface requires a new file in our program; we will create one called Tank.java. If you are using an IDE, make sure you create it as an interface file and not as a class file:

```java
public interface Tank {
}
```

This is not a class, but is instead an interface, defined by the interface clause on the first line.

Interfaces are built differently than classes. Interfaces don't have constructors, and you only need to provide the public methods that a class that implements the interface needs to have to make it "legal" to implement. The methods don't need to have any code in them, and they don't need to include access modifiers; it is just used as a reference check for Java to know that what you are creating and assigning to an interface typed container is valid.

Our Fighter and Paladin classes contain two public methods, showStats() and addXP(), so we need to add those definitions in the interface:

```java
public interface Tank {
    void showStats();
    void addXP(int deltaXP);
}
```

That is all we need to create in our interface file, but now we need to implement it on a class. Let's start with the Fighter.

To implement an interface, you need to add the implement statement and the name of the interface that you are applying to the class in the first line of the code:

```java
public class Fighter extends PlayerCharacter implements Tank {
```

That's it! Now we can go back to our Party class and type to our new interface:

```
public class Party {

    Tank tank;

    Party() {}
}
```

You'll see that the code doesn't show any errors, and the new container will accept anything that implements the Tank interface.

We can update the Paladin class in the same way:

```
public class Paladin extends PlayerCharacter implements Tank {
```

When you implement an interface, you can implement more than one with a class. So for the Paladin, when the Healer interface is created, you would add that after Tank, adding a comma in between them.

Now we can create instances of Fighter and Paladin to include in our program:

```
public class Party {

    Tank tank;

    Party() {
        tank = new Fighter("Sentri");
        tank = new Paladin("Dupre");
        tank = new Mage("Jaana");
    }
}
```

In the preceding code, the Fighter and Paladin instances are legal, because they implement the Tank interface. The Mage, however, generates an error, because the class does not implement the interface.

We can now create public and private access modifiers to our Party class. First, we need to make the container private and then create a public method to allow us to add a character to the slot in the party:

```
public class Party {

    private Tank tank;

    Party() {}

    public void addTank(Tank pc) {
        tank = pc;
        System.out.println("Tank added to party.");
    }
}
```

Now we can replace our code in Main with our new Party class:

```
public class Main {

    public static void main(String[] args) {
        Party myParty = new Party();
        myParty.addTank(new Fighter("Sentri"));
    }
}
```

If we run this program, we will see the following message:

```
A new fighter named Sentri has been created!
Tank added to party.

Process finished with exit code 0
```

Interfaces can be considered categories for your classes. You define what those category requirements are in the interface and then tell your classes that they are part of the category by implementing the interface for it.

All I'm Getting Is Static

When we work with classes and instances of these classes, we have members, or fields and methods, that are exclusive to each of the instances, but are defined by the classes. There are times where we might want to have fields and methods be the same across all instances of classes or to have a way to call methods from a class without needing to create an instance of it. That can be done by creating static fields and methods in our classes.

In our program, each of the character subclasses of Mage, Paladin, Priest, and Fighter builds the values for the skill attributes by adding a value from a virtual die to a base value. We can take this code and put it in a class called Die and then create a static method so we don't need to create an instance of the Die class. This is helpful for when you need to create methods that are tools and universal in your program but don't require instances to be able to call them.

We start by creating a Die class like we have with the previous classes:

```java
public class Die {
    public static int roll(int d) {
        int num = (int) (Math.random() * d) + 1;
        return num;
    }
}
```

The method we have created here, roll, has been defined using the static keyword after public. This makes this method available to anyone that calls it from the Die class itself, not from an instance.

So in our Mage class, for instance, we can now call this method within our constructor and pass in the number of sides on this virtual die:

© Doug Winnie 2021
D. Winnie, *Essential Java for AP CompSci*, https://doi.org/10.1007/978-1-4842-6183-5_59

```
Mage(String newName) {
    super();
    // Constructor
    name = newName;

    strength = 7;
    intelligence = 15;
    agility = 8;

    wisdom = 10;

    strength += Die.roll(6);
    intelligence += Die.roll(6);
    agility += Die.roll(6);
    wisdom += Die.roll(6);

    calcHPMP();

    xp = 0;
    level = 1;

    System.out.println("A new mage named " + name + " has been created!");
}
```

We didn't need to create an instance of the Die class, simply called the static method that is defined in the class itself.

Now, I can always create an instance of the Die class if I wish:

```
Die myDie = new Die();
int val = myDie.roll(6);
```

But there isn't a compelling need to create an instance of this class. To prevent this, we can redefine our class to be an abstract class. That way, we can't inadvertently create an instance of it and still have access to the various static methods that we can use as tools within our program.

But we can also create static fields in our classes. Static fields differ from regular fields in that the value is the same across all instances of the class. For example, if we create two mages, each one will have a unique value for their ability attributes, experience, and other values that are inside of it. If we create a static field in the Mage class, as we change that value, it will be the same across all instances of the class.

In our program, we can create a static variable that will store how many characters have been created in the game. We can define this in the PlayerCharacter superclass, so it will count for each instance of a class that extends from this class.

We use the static keyword just like we did with the Die class, but in this case we are creating a field. Since we want this available to all of the subclasses, we use the protected access modifier:

```
public abstract class PlayerCharacter {
    // Name
    protected String name;

    // Skill attributes
    protected int strength;
    protected int intelligence;
    protected int agility;

    // Health and magic
    protected int maxHitPoints;
    protected int hitPoints;
    protected int maxMana;
    protected int mana;

    // Experience
    protected int xp;
    protected int level;

    // Player Count
    protected static int pcCount = 0;

    PlayerCharacter() {}

    protected void showStats() {}

    protected void addXP(int deltaXP) {
        if (deltaXP < 0) {
            System.out.println("ERROR: Invalid experience delta value");
            return;
        }
```

```
        xp += deltaXP;
        level = (int) (xp / 1000) + 1;
    }
}
```

The intent of this field will be to hold the total number of characters we have in the game. So we can increment this value each time the PlayerCharacter constructor is run, since that will run along with the constructor of the subclass upon instantiation:

```
PlayerCharacter() {
    pcCount++;
}
```

Since we are doing this in the constructor, I need to make sure I define the value of pcCount before construction, so that is why it is defined at the top of the class.

Next, I can create a static method that will return the value of this when asked by the program. Since I need this accessible for the subclasses (since those are the actual classes being instantiated), I need to mark it as protected and static:

```
protected static int numPC() {
    return pcCount;
}
```

Now, this method can be called from any instance or from the superclass itself. Let's test it out and see how it works. We can update our Main class like this:

```
public class Main {

    public static void main(String[] args) {
        Party myParty = new Party();
        myParty.addTank(new Fighter("Sentri"));
        myParty.addRange(new Mage("Jaana"));
        myParty.addHealer(new Paladin("Dupre"));

        PlayerCharacter p1 = new Mage("Merlin");

        System.out.println("There are now " + p1.numPC() + " players in
        the game");
    }
}
```

When I create the p1 character, based on the Mage class, I have four characters created in the game. So when Sentri, Jaana, Dupre, and Merlin are all created, the pcCount static field has been incremented four times, so the value should be four:

```
A new fighter named Sentri has been created!
Tank added to party.
A new mage named Jaana has been created!
Range added to party.
A new paladin named Dupre has been created!
Healer added to party.
A new mage named Merlin has been created!
There are now 4 players in the game

Process finished with exit code 0
```

We can see that is exactly what happens when we run the program. Even though each character instance has their own attributes and other individual values, the pcCount field, since it was marked static, is shared and the same across all instances of classes that extend the superclass.

If we add a second character after the p1 character:

```
PlayerCharacter p2 = new Paladin("Francisco");
```

We can then test this by asking both p1 and p2 how many players are in the game:

```
System.out.println("There are now " + p1.numPC() + " players in the game");
System.out.println("There are now " + p2.numPC() + " players in the game");
```

When we run the program, we see

```
A new fighter named Sentri has been created!
Tank added to party.
A new mage named Jaana has been created!
Range added to party.
A new paladin named Dupre has been created!
Healer added to party.
A new mage named Merlin has been created!
A new paladin named Francisco has been created!
```

```
There are now 5 players in the game
There are now 5 players in the game

Process finished with exit code 0
```

So each instance, even when asked individually, returns the same value since it was marked static.

Finally, we can also call this from the PlayerCharacter class itself, since we created this as a static method of the class:

```
System.out.println("There are now " + PlayerCharacter.numPC() + " players in the game");
```

This returns the same value as the previous two.

Static class members, including fields and methods, are tools to help keep consistency of data across class instances and give you direct access to methods and actions that don't need to have instances to make them work in your program.

An All-Star Cast, Featuring Null

With most of the program finished, we only have a few more things to wrap up. We have a party system built into our program, but we need a way to work with that collection of players in our Party class and work with them as a group in our main program. Along the way, we will encounter a few other items we need to accommodate for in our program.

Let's first take a look at our existing program in the Main class:

```java
public class Main {

    public static void main(String[] args) {
        Party myParty = new Party();
        myParty.addTank(new Fighter("Sentri"));
        myParty.addRange(new Mage("Jaana"));
        myParty.addHealer(new Paladin("Dupre"));
    }
}
```

We have added three characters into our party, but once they are in the party, there isn't much we can do with them. The first thing we would want to do is show the stats for each of the characters in the various slots. We can create a public method to show their stats.

If we go to the Party class, we can add the method there:

```java
public void showParty() {
    tank.showStats();
    range.showStats();
    healer.showStats();
}
```

© Doug Winnie 2021
D. Winnie, *Essential Java for AP CompSci*, https://doi.org/10.1007/978-1-4842-6183-5_60

This would work in our program as designed, but if we removed one of the characters, we would get an error:

```
public class Main {

    public static void main(String[] args) {
        Party myParty = new Party();
        myParty.addTank(new Fighter("Sentri"));
        myParty.addRange(new Mage("Jaana"));
        // myParty.addHealer(new Paladin("Dupre"));
    }
}
```

Now we have removed a character from a slot. When we attempt to run the program, we will get an error:

```
Exception in thread "main" java.lang.NullPointerException
```

A null pointer exception means that we are attempting to access a named value, in this case a field called healer, but it doesn't have a value associated with it or is valued as null. When we attempt to access it, we get this error.

We can gracefully test if a value is null to avoid this issue. We would build a series of conditional statements to ask if the value is equal to the statement null. Null is a special value that exists when a field is created, but has no value. We have that situation in our Party class instance when we first create it, because we create the containers for tank, healer, and range at the top of the class, but we don't populate them with values until the program adds a new PlayerCharacter subclass instance to each of the slots.

We can update our showParty method with tests for null:

```
public void showParty() {
    if (tank == null) {
        System.out.println("No tank is assigned in the party!");
    } else {
        System.out.println("Party Tank:");
        tank.showStats();
    }
```

```java
if (range == null) {
    System.out.println("No range is assigned in the party!");
} else {
    System.out.println("Party Range:");
    range.showStats();
}

if (healer == null) {
    System.out.println("No healer is assigned in the party!");
} else {
    System.out.println("Party Healer:");
    healer.showStats();
}
}
```

Now, in each party slot, we first ask if the named container lacks any value by asking if it is equal to null. If it is null, we display a message. If it does contain a value, we then execute the showStats method for that character:

```
A new fighter named Sentri has been created!
Tank added to party.
A new mage named Jaana has been created!
Range added to party.

Party Tank:
-----------------------------------
Sentri, a level 1 fighter with 0 XP:
STR: 19 | INT: 8 | AGI: 10 | CON: 13 | HP: 64 / 64 | MP: 0 / 0

Party Range:
-----------------------------------
Jaana, a level 1 mage with 0 XP:
STR: 10 | INT: 17 | AGI: 10 | WIS: 13 | HP: 10 / 10 | MP: 43 / 43

No healer is assigned in the party!
```

Now we avoid a null pointer exception by testing for null in each instance.

Let's uncomment the healer and add the next part of the program.

We need to have a way to access the various characters in our party. One way to do that is to create a collection and return that as a public method of the Party class. Then we can build a loop that will go through each of the items in our party.

First, we need to create the public method that will build and return an ArrayList of PlayerCharacters, populated with each of the party slots:

```
public ArrayList<PlayerCharacter> getParty() {
    ArrayList<PlayerCharacter> myParty = new ArrayList<PlayerCharacter>();
    myParty.add(tank);
    myParty.add(range);
    myParty.add(healer);
    return myParty;
}
```

When we create this code, we get a syntax error. The reason is that tank, range, and healer are all typed to interfaces. Our ArrayList, myParty, is typed with PlayerCharacter, so they don't match.

But we know that they actually are the same; we just have an issue where they aren't strict matches to the types that are being asked for. How do we solve this? We can use a cast.

We have used casts to convert numbers and evaluations into specific data types, like integers. We can also do that with our own classes when we know that they are actually the same type. We can update our code to cast each of the interface typed containers to PlayerCharacter types:

```
public ArrayList<PlayerCharacter> getParty() {
    ArrayList<PlayerCharacter> myParty = new ArrayList<PlayerCharacter>();
    myParty.add((PlayerCharacter) tank);
    myParty.add((PlayerCharacter) range);
    myParty.add((PlayerCharacter) healer);
    return myParty;
}
```

Now our method will work since all of the types explicitly match.

Back to our main program, we can then work with this new public method and simulate turns that earn experience points. I'll display the stats of the party at the beginning of the program, generate experience, and then display the stats at the end:

```java
public class Main {

    public static void main(String[] args) {
        Party myParty = new Party();
        myParty.addTank(new Fighter("Sentri"));
        myParty.addRange(new Mage("Jaana"));
        myParty.addHealer(new Paladin("Dupre"));

        // At start of game
        System.out.println("START OF GAME:\n");
        myParty.showParty();

        int turns = 20;
        for (int i = 1; i <= turns; i++) {
            for (PlayerCharacter pc : myParty.getParty())
                if (pc != null) pc.addXP((int) (Math.random() * 1000));
        }

        // At end of game
        System.out.println("END OF GAME:\n");
        myParty.showParty();

    }
}
```

We create a variable to indicate how many turns we want to generate, and then we want to loop through each of the characters in our party. We can do that because we have the getParty method that will return an ArrayList collection of all of the party members. With each of those members, we want to make sure they aren't null and then add a random amount of experience points.

When we run the program, we get our party stats with the simulated experience:

```
A new fighter named Sentri has been created!
Tank added to party.
A new mage named Jaana has been created!
Range added to party.
A new paladin named Dupre has been created!
Healer added to party.
START OF GAME:
```

Party Tank:

Sentri, a level 1 fighter with 0 XP:

STR: 20 | INT: 11 | AGI: 14 | CON: 16 | HP: 72 / 72 | MP: 0 / 0

Party Range:

Jaana, a level 1 mage with 0 XP:

STR: 10 | INT: 19 | AGI: 11 | WIS: 15 | HP: 10 / 10 | MP: 49 / 49

Party Healer:

Dupre, a level 1 paladin with 0 XP:

STR: 15 | INT: 21 | AGI: 8 | WIS: 16 | CON: 12 | HP: 39 / 39 | MP: 53 / 53

END OF GAME:

Party Tank:

Sentri, a level 9 fighter with 8615 XP:

STR: 21 | INT: 15 | AGI: 16 | CON: 17 | HP: 76 / 76 | MP: 0 / 0

Party Range:

Jaana, a level 13 mage with 12058 XP:

STR: 13 | INT: 20 | AGI: 14 | WIS: 20 | HP: 13 / 13 | MP: 60 / 60

Party Healer:

Dupre, a level 11 paladin with 10814 XP:

STR: 16 | INT: 22 | AGI: 11 | WIS: 20 | CON: 13 | HP: 42 / 42 | MP: 62 / 62

When you create classes that contain fields that are not immediately initialized, we need to remember to account for that by testing for null values to avoid issues. When we start mixing superclasses, subclasses, and interfaces, we are sometimes faced with a situation where types don't strictly match. By using casts, we can overcome that limitation when we know that the underlying values do in fact match.

Index

A

Abstract clause, 288
Abstract, 255
add() method, 230
addAll() method, 232
addXP() method, 296, 299
Algebraic order of operations, 93
Algorithm, 16
Analytical engine, 13
ArrayList
    add items, 230
    clear() method, 232
    coding, 233, 234
    collection, 284, 286
    copy elements, 232
    creation, 229
    find items, 231
    generics, 235, 237, 238
    get elements, 230
    looping, 239, 240
    remove elements, 231
    replace items, 232
    size() method, 232
    without generics, 243, 284
Arrays
    coding, 212, 213
    creation
        by size, 210
        delimited list, 216
        with values, 209
    getting value, 210
    looping, 211
    nested loops, 225
    number of values, 211
    pitfalls, 210
ASCII + unicode, 88
Assignment operator, 209
Automatic program loop, 183, 185
average() method, 127

B

Backup, 10
Binary number
    bit sizes, 81
    counting to "10", 78
    vs. decimal, 77, 79
    overflow, 84
    store values, 81
    unsigned and signed
        numbers, 83
Blocks, 50
Boolean evaluation, 142
Boolean logic code, 143–145
Boolean logic operators, 142
Boolean values, 142
Boolean variables, 141
Byte, 75

© Doug Winnie 2021
D. Winnie, *Essential Java for AP CompSci*, https://doi.org/10.1007/978-1-4842-6183-5

Printed in the United States
by Baker & Taylor Publisher Services